CHECKMATE

CHECKMATE

TIPS & LESSONS TO HELP YOU MAKE THE RIGHT MOVES TO ACHIEVE HAPPINESS!

GREG DAVIS

To Abby, thanks for allowing me to follow my crazy dreams and joining me as my queen in my chess game of life. Thanks for being my inspiration and my motivation to keep moving forward. Keep dreaming, shining, and spreading your love. Your presence makes this world better.

I love you with all my heart.

CONTENTS

———

INTRODUCTION

———

Why was a fifty-three-year-old man sitting alone in a hotel room on a warm Monday night in California 3,000 miles from home, crying like a baby?

For me, life resembles a game of chess. We make many choices throughout our lives related to our careers, finding a life partner, where to live, and financial issues such as developing a budget or how much to save for retirement. Ultimately, a game of chess ends in a checkmate when your opponent's king has no possible escape. In this book, you will discover how and why I made some of my moves in life to accomplish my form of checkmate, which was to achieve happiness.

On June 30, 2013, my boss, Dave, shared the surprise news of my difficult decision to retire from the world-renowned hospitality company Hershey Entertainment and Resorts (HE&R) after twenty-three years of working for this well-run organization. I moved up the ranks of the finance department to my final position as associate vice president of finance. A good friend and coworker, Frank O'Connell, died in October 2011 at the early age of forty-eight due to a heart attack. After his untimely death, my wife, Abby, and I decided to reevaluate our priorities. Abby was a busy pathologist for a regional hospital in York, Pennsylvania, so we decided to exit our high-stress jobs and move into an early retirement phase. This would allow us to spend more time together and do things we felt were beneficial to others, like teaching and volunteering.

The stress and long hours became harmful to our health. While we were both making a good income, we hoped this was the change and fulfillment our life needed. I had become a bit burned out in the hectic corporate world, even though I loved the company and my coworkers. Abby felt the same in medicine, with even longer hours and higher stress than I had. Unfortunately, it took the untimely passing of our dear friend, Frank, to lead us to another path in life. In an odd way, Frank's death reinvigorated our life.

From a financial standpoint, Abby and I had done all the right things to build a healthy retirement nest. I will share some tips and practices from my three years of writing a personal finance blog later in this book. Our years of saving and investing allowed us greater flexibility to seek other opportunities and rewards than what our current jobs offered. Abby wanted to pursue other benevolent activities, such as volunteering. As we will see, family and personal events prevented her from fulfilling this desire until we later moved to Philadelphia. Since I had loved teaching college courses as an adjunct professor, I decided teaching on a full-time basis was my calling. Based on my adjunct teaching experience, numerous accounting certifications, and thirty-three years of business experience, I thought getting a full-time college teaching position would be easy. As I discovered, I was wrong.

I reached out to fifteen colleges and universities on the East Coast only to get fourteen refusals and just one interview with Penn State University (PSU) for a teaching position at a local campus. The interview went poorly due to the heavy focus on my not having a PhD. I quickly realized I had screwed up by underestimating the importance of this degree in my academic job search.

While I came up empty on the East Coast over the summer of 2013, an academic conference on the West Coast provided another job opportunity. In August 2013, I boarded an airplane to fly across the country to attend the largest worldwide annual accounting teacher conference hosted by the American Accounting Association in Anaheim, California. While the annual conference included presentations on numerous industry topics, my primary goal was to network with other professors and attend the job fair. To participate in the conference job fair, I sent my application materials (résumé, teaching philosophy, etc.) several weeks before the conference so hiring institutions could review the candidate information in advance.

A week later, the assistant to the accountancy department chair from the University of Illinois at Urbana-Champaign contacted me. They liked my background from the job fair materials and wanted to know if I had "any free time" for an interview with them on Monday night of the conference. While trying to act coy, I indicated I "could fit them in," even though I had no other interviews scheduled.

I arrived in Los Angeles on Sunday afternoon only to discover the airline lost my luggage. *Okay*, I thought, as I needed to stay calm. On Monday, my first day of the four-day conference, I had no luck making any connections in academia for other job fair interviews. After several frustrating calls with the airline, I discovered they were continuing to locate my luggage. I persuaded the airline to provide me with a credit to buy some clothes just in time for my interview with Illinois.

As I returned to my hotel room after the dreadful first day of the conference on a warm muggy day, I opened an email from a good friend of mine at HE&R. Garrett explained how much he and the company would miss me and my supportive style of leadership. He went on to urge me to return to HE&R if things did not work out in my academic job search. After reading his email and realizing how much I missed Abby, I started sobbing uncontrollably. After working almost half my life at HE&R and working my way up the corporate ladder, my thoughts revolved around whether I was making a big mistake by walking away from my business career and starting a new one in academia at age fifty-three.

After my panic attack subsided and I washed the tears from my face, my fortunes began to change. The interview went well as the department chair, Jon Davis, indicated Illinois was looking to hire professionally oriented faculty, defined as "faculty from professional backgrounds who primarily contribute in teaching and service, with a limited research focus." While I did not have the PhD degree that East Coast colleges required, my experience at Hershey was attractive to Illinois to bring valuable real-world experience to the classroom and their students. After discussing my experience and various accounting certifications, Jon invited me to a fall campus visit in Champaign, Illinois. After the disappointment over the past several months, I was stunned at how well the interview had gone. Based on my recent debacle with the PSU interview, I was also a bit skeptical.

After crying in my hotel room and wondering whether I may have made a huge mistake in leaving HE&R and changing professions at age fifty-three, I decided someday to write a book about my life experiences. I was hopeful my book would encourage others to achieve their dreams and increase their happiness.

Happiness is a combination of factors that is hard to achieve, especially during these trying times. Take a look at these current statistics:

1. Only 19 percent of American adults say they are very happy. We struggle with being happy. The worldwide pandemic is partially to blame as this is way down from 31 percent of adults who said the same in 2018 (Ingraham 2022).
2. Sixty percent of American workers are actively searching for a new job, according to Fortune (Leonhardt 2021). While higher pay is the primary reason, improved benefits and career advancement are other reasons for this prominent level of job-hopping.
3. Thirty-two percent of Americans cannot pull together $400 to cover an emergency (Adamczyk 2022). We need to learn better ways to determine how we use and save our money.

4. Per the US Census Bureau, while 68 percent of Americans have access to employer-sponsored 401(k) plans, only 41 percent contribute to their retirement plan (Deer 2022). This shortfall results in Americans leaving a staggering twenty-four billion in unclaimed 401(k) company matches on the table each year (Jurs 2015).

As indicated by these depressing statistics, we need help to be happier. My story will reflect my path to happiness.

The good news is that I finally got my luggage back on Wednesday, three days after my arrival in Los Angeles. The best news occurred a few weeks later when Jon's assistant called to arrange the campus visit to Illinois, as we had discussed at the job fair. Abby and I flew to Champaign, Illinois, and enjoyed walking around campus over the weekend before my grueling all-day interview on Monday, October 19, 2013.

My interview process was extremely tiring. I met numerous Gies College of Business faculty. I also gave a thirty-minute teaching demonstration in front of the head, Jon Davis, and three other faculty members from the accountancy department. After the interview, I met Abby in the hotel lobby as she was her usual supportive self in this crazy quest of mine. The long day exhausted me, yet I was hopeful I had done well. I appreciated meeting the impressive faculty. Abby had enjoyed walking around the beautiful campus with the autumn colors. About five weeks later, I received the job offer to be a full-time accountancy lecturer at the University of Illinois at Urbana-Champaign, starting in the fall of 2014. Thanks to Abby's amazing support throughout my journey, we achieved the goal that we mutually established in 2011.

Perseverance is the key to achieving your dreams, even if it means overcoming lots of obstacles along the way. As John D. Rockefeller said, "I do not think there is any quality so essential to success of any kind as the quality of perseverance. It overcomes almost everything, even nature" (Marden 1901). I was able to complete this career change because Abby and I were prepared financially for a lifestyle change. While most American high schools or colleges do not teach personal finance, we need to learn some key aspects on our own, which you will do in my book.

You may be thinking, *Who is this book designed to help?* I feel this book would greatly benefit anyone considering or experiencing a transition in their life, such as a career change, contemplating retirement, or other life-altering events.

Why should you read this book? Through my examples, you will learn:

- How to overcome obstacles (e.g., job stress and grief from the loss of family members and friends), step outside your comfort zone, and achieve happiness in your life.
- Best practices to change careers and realize your true passions (e.g., What is it like to teach or mentor others?).
- Concepts on how to budget and save your money today, leading to an enriched retirement phase later in your life.
- How to stop worrying about financial topics and have positive conversations with your spouse on a regular basis.
- Ways to achieve greater happiness in your life.

Despite facing many obstacles in my career change at age fifty-three, I persevered and fulfilled my dream of teaching at the college level while increasing our happiness as a couple. I had no idea I would teach at the prestigious University of Illinois for the next seven years and have the most rewarding experiences of my forty-year career. Let us continue our journey together as I cannot wait to share my story of how I played my chess game of life by making the right moves and, occasionally, the *wrong* ones as well. As a professor, I need you to pay attention, as there will be a homework assignment at the end of this book. Enjoy the journey and determine how you can apply my lessons to increase happiness in your life.

CHAPTER 1:

CHERISH FAMILY TIME!

Family is not an important thing. It's everything.

—MICHAEL J. FOX

While you can define family in many ways, I feel our family upbringing is the key to who we are as adults and, in many ways, the main driver of our happiness. While the definition of American families is changing, they provide the most pleasure in our busy lives.

Per a *US News & World Report* article, "The percentage of married adults dropped from 1960 to 2008 from 72 percent to 52 percent. The percentage of people separated or divorced nearly tripled over this time. Even as marriage shrinks, family—in all its emerging varieties—remains resilient." The rise of new family structures and public attitudes toward marriage and family indicates that "roughly 75 percent of adults consider their own family to be the most important, most satisfying element of their lives" (Moeller 2012). I firmly believe family, while trying at times, is the bedrock upon which we build a healthy and happy life.

I was born in the Carlisle Hospital in Pennsylvania on December 15, 1959, as the youngest of five children. My family raised me on a farm outside the small town of York Springs. I grew up in a loving yet poor family as I wore my brother's hand-me-down clothes until I was ten years old. Unfortunately, in the summer of 1962, one of my older brothers, Bobby, died tragically in a tractor accident at the age of sixteen when one of the back wheels came off his tractor and caused it to roll over. I do not recall many memories of Bobby or the horrific accident, as I was only two years old. My siblings told me Bobby had an endearing personality and looked like me. My family took this accident as a sign that we should exit the career of farming and start a new life in a different setting.

As it turns out, this is not the only time a vehicle accident would claim the life of one of my brothers.

My dad was a hard worker, and he worked three jobs to save enough money to buy a new house. In addition to farming, he drove a bus for our school district. Then at night, he worked as a security guard at Gettysburg College. While my dad did not make much money in this security guard position, he was able to send three of his children—my sister, Shirley, my brother, Doug, and me—to this great liberal arts private college for negligible tuition cost. To this day, I am thankful for the excellent education I received from this exceptional small college.

At the age of five, my family moved away from the farm. My entire family was excited when we moved into our new stone house. One of my worst memories of my childhood occurred on the first day we visited the large house before the movers arrived with our furniture. When I saw the expansive living room, I became exuberant and tossed a full bottle of milk across the room to Doug after he had persuaded me to throw it. Unfortunately, he failed to catch the glass milk bottle. I watched in horror as the top came flying off the bottle and milk spilled out over our newly carpeted living room. Visibly upset, my dad sent both Doug and me to bed after paddling us, which led to lots of crying and sore butts for both of us. This occasion was the only time my dad or mom ever laid a hand on my brother or me. Oddly enough, I have never drunk a glass of milk since that fateful day.

My stay-at-home mother had one of the most difficult jobs of all, especially with five kids running around the house. Shirley was the oldest child and my only sister, as we are sixteen years apart. We remain close, and she has done a lot for many family members over the years. My oldest brother, Harold Jr. (June), was the clown of the family, as he was well known for his practical jokes. Being the baby of the family, I stuck close to my brother, Doug, who was only four years older than me.

Doug was popular and smart, as he was president and vale-dictorian of his high school class and achieved high grades during his years at Gettysburg College, where he worked hard for his impressive grades. Thus, he set an exceedingly high standard for me and made me want to exert myself to try to match his outstanding achievements. Doug worked for many Fortune 500 companies (e.g., RCA, Hershey Company, General Foods) as a successful information technology (IT) specialist. His favorite job was working for his alma mater,

Gettysburg College, for the admissions department in his final years before his untimely passing in the fall of 2020.

It appears that writing was in my blood from an early age. My sister-in-law, Lynn, found my first written document in April 2022 in one of Doug's family heirloom boxes, which was a three-page masterpiece written for a fifth-grade assignment. As per my autobiography, "I vividly remember the surprise I felt at age seven. Shirley bought me my first new bike at Easter. That same Easter, my dad also bought two pet baby rabbits for Doug and me. Doug's bunny was white and named Thumper. Mine was gray and named Grayhound" (Davis 1969). This would begin an era of incredibly brilliant naming conventions for our pets. On this topic, my autobiography indicates, "I received a brown, black, and white spotted beagle puppy, which I called Spotty." Later I creatively named pets Fluffy, Browny, and Blacky. These pet name examples are why Abby has named all our pets.

My autobiography indicates, "In fourth grade, my teacher was Miss Shirley Davis, which was unique as she is my sister. While it sounds like an easy year of being taught by your oldest sibling, it was an incredibly challenging year for me. Shirley pushed both my best friend, Kai, and me to work harder as we learned to challenge ourselves to be better students. I felt good about the year, as I learned a lot from my sister.

While I was fortunate to grow up in such a large and loving family with many pets, my siblings taught me that hard work is the most reliable path to success. June was the only child who did not go to college and yet became one of the most successful family members as he worked himself from being a janitor just out of high school to being a well-respected senior manager for a Fortune 500 company, Tyco, for over forty years. Shirley was a beloved elementary schoolteacher at Bermudian Springs School District for thirty-one years. My older siblings were loyal, hard-working members of their organizations. Loyalty and hard work went together for the Davis family, which taught me the value of these traits. I firmly believe these factors led to my successful forty-year career in the field of accounting. In a March 2022 interview with Shirley, I wanted to get her perspective on growing up as the oldest sibling in our family. She replied, "We were a very loving family but a poor family. We were farmers, but we all worked hard, and that is part of our life. We learned great work ethic even at the early age of five or six."

As we know too well, not all of life is happy.

"The loss of a loved one is life's most stressful event and can cause a major emotional crisis as we experience bereavement, which means 'to be deprived by death'" (MHA n.d.). Let us get this out on the table in the first chapter: I am horrible at dealing with grief, as I tend to suppress my feelings. While you never stop missing your loved ones, the pain eases after time and allows you to move on with your life. Losing a family member or a close friend is painful, and those feelings intensify when you lose three family members over the course of ten months!

On the morning of Friday, March 13, 2020 (Friday the thirteenth for us superstitious folks), I was excited to start the spring break portion of my semester at the University of Illinois. Many Americans will remember this fateful day as the start of the COVID-19 pandemic in the US, as it was on this day that President Donald Trump declared a nationwide emergency, and the world has changed ever since. Despite the pandemic, Abby and I had decided to drive back to Pennsylvania to visit family and friends as we normally do on my college breaks. Our main agenda was to visit our brother-in-law, Wayne, who was in his final months of care at the Carlisle Hospital. After a long drive, we arrived on Saturday morning to see Wayne and my sister, Shirley, his loving wife of forty years. However, the hospital was restricting patient visits due to the start of the COVID-19 pandemic. While prohibited inside his room, we could see Wayne from the hallway to see his warm face and speak with him briefly. We were very fortunate to visit Wayne that day, as the hospital restricted all visitors the next day. We were able to see Wayne one last time before he passed away less than a month later in April.

In September 2020, it was a beautiful sunny day as I was driving home to have lunch with Abby. My work week was over, and we looked forward to a nice fall weekend. As we were enjoying our lunch, I received a phone call from Doug's wife of twenty-nine years, Lynn. Upon answering, I was a bit concerned since I did not receive many phone calls directly from her as Doug was the main conduit for family related information. She validated my concerns when she explained a motor vehicle accident tragically killed Doug on his drive to work at Gettysburg College. This news was particularly upsetting to me. I was very close to Doug, and we enjoyed going to baseball games and dinner together. In May 2022, Lynn gave me one of Doug's baseball caps that I gave to him when I started teaching at the University of Illinois. While it may seem silly, I love wearing this cap as it brings back great memories of the many baseball games Doug and I attended together!

After I made some arrangements for the next week within my accounting department, Abby and I drove back to Pennsylvania the next morning. Due to some amazing professors on our intermediate accounting team, I was able to take a week off from my Illinois classes to be with my family. While the week was difficult under the circumstances, I was grateful to be able to spend an entire week with family and attend Doug's funeral services a week after the accident that took his life. The highlight was spending quality time with Doug's two wonderful daughters, Kristi and Kylee. Despite the sudden and unexpected loss of their sixty-five-year-old dad, they showed resilience and loving kindness during a horrible grief-stricken period. While Kylee is currently a high school teacher, Kristi has worked in the medical and fitness fields and is the proud mother of a beautiful baby boy, Alexander, born in September 2021. Doug would have been an amazing grandfather.

We will remember the year 2020 as a challenging year for many people. Our lives changed dramatically with the onset of the COVID-19 pandemic in March of that year. Holiday visits with family members outside your immediate household would have to wait. A longtime smoker, my oldest brother, June, was fighting heart disease for a long time and beginning to slow down as the holidays approached. I spoke with him as often as possible during his final weeks. With his loving wife of fifty-six years, Linda, and sister, Shirley, by his side, he entered into eternal peace in January 2021. In typical fashion for this very gracious and grateful man, June's last words were, "Thank you." I have kept several of June's voice-mails on my cell phone as a memory of our last conversations.

Many of us will remember the COVID-19 pandemic for how it changed our lives in more ways than we could have imagined. My heart goes out to the many families who lost family members to this horrible virus. As of September 2022, there have been "over one million deaths in the United States from this dreaded virus" (CDC 2022). As Abby so eloquently wrote in our year-end 2020 holiday letter, "God has called more people back home than typical for the year."

For the rest of the Davis family and me, we will remember it as a particularly challenging ten-month period from April 2020 through January 2021. We lost three amazing male members of our family: Wayne, Doug, and June. Between them, they were fortunate to have enjoyed 125 years of marriage to their loving wives: Shirley, Lynn, and Linda. As Abby wrote in our 2020 holiday letter, "Tomorrow is promised to no one."

In a particularly emotional story from an interesting TEDx Talk, Dominic Price (Dom is a work futurist) relates the amazing story of "his sister dying in his arms at age forty-five of Stage 4 breast cancer" (2021). As death sometimes does, it made me think with renewed clarity about life, work, and all the things that mattered in my life and made me happy.

In all honesty, I have some regrets about working in Illinois and being 700 miles away during this challenging period for my family in Pennsylvania. From time to time, we get so caught up in our work and busy schedules that we forget some of life's simple pleasures, such as family time. I enjoyed reading a book by Bonnie Ware, *The Top Five Regrets of Dying*, where Bonnie shared with her readers one of the biggest regrets of people she has cared for under hospice situations, "I wish I hadn't spent so much time in the office" (Ware 2019).

It made me rethink the purpose of Abby and me working sixty to seventy hours per week during the peak years of our careers, which led to one of the most difficult decisions of our lives in 2014. As I mentioned, we both left our rewarding careers and moved to the college town of Champaign, Illinois, so I could pursue my passion for teaching (much like seven members of our collective families who are or were devoted teachers). While some people thought the idea was crazy, it is one of the best decisions we made as a couple, as the new lifestyle allowed us to spend more time together and enjoy greater happiness.

My favorite takeaway from his TEDx Talk is when Dom discusses what is "really important to all of us on our deathbed is the love of friends and family, the legacy you are leaving behind, knowing you have done things that make you and others happy" (Price 2021). By working closely with our trusted financial advisor and friend, Tom Zielinski, from the Royal Bank of Canada (RBC), and following some of the finance tips shared later in this book, we were able to leave our major careers and be fully retired at age fifty-five and sixty-one, respectively, for Abby and me. After seven years of teaching and living in Illinois, we love being back in Pennsylvania. We have increased our happiness by spending more time with family and friends, doing more things together, and working on the legacy we wish to leave behind.

Abby and I are the queen and king in our chess game of life, and our family and close friends are the remaining key pieces. Unfortunately, my family lost three key pieces during the tumultuous period of 2020 to 2021 when God called for my two brothers, June and Doug, as well as my gentle giant of a brother-in-law, Wayne. As in chess, when we lose our pieces, the game of life moves on. I still have pleasant memories of my brothers and enjoy seeing pictures of them and Wayne in our various family albums. Take a moment to reflect on the fond memories of those family members you have lost, and be sure to cherish the time you spend with your family.

Despite the many time constraints in our busy lives, my recommendation heavily gears toward spending more time with family. Keep in mind this chapter's lesson: *Never regret spending time with your family, and remember those who leave us.*

CHAPTER 2:

RELATIONSHIPS

"Every thirteen seconds, a couple in the US is breaking up."

This shocking statement came from a TEDx Talk by Maya Diamond, an expert dating and relationship coach known for helping people finally find the loving partner they have been seeking. In her TEDx Talk, I learned that "lifetime relationships all have one thing in common: emotional responsiveness, which contains three crucial elements" (2019).

1. Accessibility: You are there when I need you.
2. Responsiveness: You can celebrate the good times with me and soothe me during difficult times.
3. Engagement: You value me, and I can feel that in our daily interactions.

Maya goes on to say, "If people gave emotional responsiveness as much weight as a hot body or a six-figure salary when choosing their life partner, there would be a lot fewer break-ups" (Diamond 2019).

This TEDx Talk made me think about how events in our lives, which we will discuss in later chapters, have impacted my relationship with Abby. While I am not perfect by any means, I tried my best to be accessible during her 2018 medical issues, responsive in celebrating her medical school graduation in 1994, and consoling her during the loss of her father and mother in 2009 and 2018, respectively, and engaging her. I value her expert opinion on many topics, which has been a huge part of my career success story.

On a recent Canadian tour, we were asked the question over dinner with three other couples, "How did you two meet?" Since my dating history is spotty at best, here is a brief synopsis of my key relationships.

In the summer of 1982, I was having lunch one day at my desk while working as a corporate analyst for Harrisburg Steel Corporation (HARSCO). My desk faced out to the swimming pool, where mostly female coworkers would enjoy their lunch while lounging around. Some would change into their swimsuits, while others would sit at the tables around the pool in their work clothes. During the summer, I began dating one of these women, Amy, and after a year we got engaged. As fate would prevail, Amy was not the one for me, as she broke up with me in 1983, just six months before our wedding date. The failure of my first love crushed me, and I realized that finding a life partner was much harder than I imagined. Although I sucked at the dating game, I went to clubs and bars for the next four years, thinking this would be where the magic would happen. I was dead wrong.

After thinking about how I met my two primary love interests, I wondered how other couples met. I found it interesting that a Stanford University survey reported an increasingly large number of daters opting to meet their partners in an online environment between 1995 and 2017 (Buchholz 2020). In a survey of over 5,400 adults, the article indicates the online method has grown from 2 percent to 39 percent, while meeting through friends, which worked well for me, grew from 20 percent to 33 percent. Surprisingly, the second most common method in recent years, meeting at bars and restaurants, did not work well for me. Lastly, meeting at work, as I did with Amy, declined from 19 percent to only 11 percent. Let us learn how I met the love of my life.

In June 1987, I played softball with a team of buddies in Hanover, Pennsylvania. I sat with two friends, Steve and Bryan, discussing our upcoming weekend plans. My best friend for forty years, Bryan, told us he was dating a softball player, Julie, and their team was having a party on Saturday night. Bryan wanted to go and asked me to tag along as his friend in case it was boring and he needed a reason to leave. I had no desire to go to a women's softball party, yet my other friend, Steve, convinced me to go as he was certain I would hit it off with Julie's best friend, Abby. I had no other weekend plans. Surprisingly, my social calendar was empty in those days as a nerdy accountant, so I decided to tag along with Bryan to the party.

The party was on Saturday, June 13, 1987, at Julie's house in West York, Pennsylvania. It offered the usual summer activities, including a cookout, volleyball, and a large keg of beer. The best part of this event was a cute girl who poured beers from the keg. Since I had made multiple stops for refills for Bryan and others on the volleyball court, I could talk with her often as she was very personable and very easy with whom to have a discussion. After finally introducing myself on my second or third trip, I realized this was the aforementioned Abby who Steve had told me about. Little did I know at that initial meeting that I would fall in love with this amazing, beautiful woman for the rest of my life.

The party progressed as Bryan and I were having a good time eating dinner and playing volleyball. I always offered to get our beers refilled, as trips to the keg became less about refilling beers and more about Abby. On these reconnaissance trips, I discovered Abby was a junior at nearby Albright College in Reading, Pennsylvania, which meant she was quite a bit younger than me, as I was twenty-seven years old. She would not be interested in an older man like me, right? Later in the evening, as Bryan and I were leaving the party, Julie indicated that Abby should join her and come along to watch some of our softball games. Much to my surprise, Abby indicated she would love to join Julie and watch our next game on the following Wednesday night. It excited me to hear the surprise news, and I could not wait to see Abby again on Wednesday.

After she attended the initial softball game, we began to see more of each other. By the time Abby returned to Albright College for her senior year, we were an item. I figured she would lose interest in the older man once she returned to campus with the young college studs, yet I was wrong. We often talked by phone and spent most weekends together. While it was a long year apart, we loved spending time together and did so whenever possible until she graduated in June 1988 with a bachelor of science in biology.

I was very happy when Abby returned to live with her parents in nearby York, Pennsylvania, after her college graduation to begin her first job as a research pharmacologist in Baltimore, Maryland. We became very close and spent most evenings and weekends together. My first *family test* occurred when her family invited me to an Independence Day picnic, where I met her mom, dad, and five siblings. While incredibly nervous, I had a blast with her personable sisters, Deb, Cindy, Cherie, and Libby, as well as her entertaining brother, Steven. Her family is a very close-knit group, not unlike my own. As is a key focus of this book, spending time with our large families became a key bonding item for Abby and me over the rest of our lives.

On the best day of my life, I married Abby Warner, my best friend, on May 19, 1990. We enjoyed an outdoor wedding at the beautiful Hershey Gardens in Hershey, Pennsylvania, and had our wedding reception at the Hershey Lodge and Convention Center. Hershey Entertainment & Resorts (HE&R) ran both of these properties. Little did I know I would work for the company, starting a year later in 1991, for over twenty-three years.

In an interview with Abby on the day of our thirty-second anniversary, May 19, 2022, I asked about her early thoughts on marriage with me. She stated, "The picture of you that came together from your interactions with friends and family and your approach toward your career helped me realize I could see myself building a life with our bond growing ever stronger."

Abby is the most intelligent person I know, as her intelligence and work ethic enabled her to fulfill her dream of becoming a doctor to help other people, which has been a consistent calling in Abby's life. After completing her rigorous five-year residency in pathology, she then completed a one-year fellowship at the prestigious University of Pennsylvania in Philadelphia in June 2000. While working in Hershey during this challenging year of living apart, I visited Abby every weekend. We fell in love with the city of Philadelphia and discussed returning to live in the city in the future. We achieved this goal a mere twenty-one years later when we moved into the Philly condominium we live in today.

When asked about my love for my wife, it is hard for me to express my true feelings. At my HE&R retirement party in January 2014, I gave a speech that included the top ten things I love about Abby. While I found it extremely difficult to discuss my love for my wife in front of my business associates and coworkers, here is what I shared:

1. Abby is very good at reading maps. This is why I refer to her as my *Ablas*.
2. She loves to watch sports with me, which is a big deal as I love baseball, football, tennis, and college basketball.
3. Abby is an incredibly supportive wife. She was a huge pillar of support during my career switch to academia.
4. She is a great cook, although we do like dining out often at good restaurants.
5. Abby is like wine, as she only gets better with age. She is much more confident in pursuing her life passions.
6. She is very smart and dedicated. See the above story on her long road to a successful career in medicine.

7. Abby is a much better basketball player than me. She played on her college team.
8. She is more attractive to me today than when I first met her. Refer back to number five.
9. Abby is fun to be with, as evidenced by our numerous fun-filled trips to Outer Banks, North Carolina (OBX), March Madness basketball tournaments, and exciting cities across the United States.
10. She makes me a better man.

I wanted to obtain a distinct perspective of Abby by interviewing her college basketball coach, Jo Ann Lightman, as Abby played basketball at Albright College. In describing Abby as a basketball player and a friend today, she said, "Abby was a thoughtful, intelligent player who earned the respect of her teammates and coach by always giving 100 percent in practice and games. She was a quiet leader, both on and off the court. Abby is truly one of my favorite athletes I have had the pleasure of coaching." It appears I am not the only person with a high opinion of Abby, as Jo Ann and the Lightman family have been some of our closest friends for the past thirty-five years. We still meet for monthly brunches.

As much as Abby and I love each other, I wondered how we became such great life partners. Reflecting on Maya Diamond's TEDx Talk on healthy relationships made me ponder why Abby and I have successfully built a lasting bond. According to US Census Bureau data, the average marriage age for Americans has increased over time.

While many of my friends married successfully in their early twenties, I waited quite a bit longer. According to a recent article, "Most Americans marry between the ages of twenty-five and thirty" (Lake 2022). I was thirty years old when we married and, in my opinion, good things take time. I feel a person should be patient and expand their boundaries to find a lifelong partner. On the other hand, I am thankful Abby had the courage at such a young age to start a relationship with an older man when she was about to embark on a successful medical career. I admire many of my friends who had the courage and conviction to marry successfully at a younger age. I was simply too immature in my twenties to settle down.

In an interesting article on best practices of married couples, I learned that even the best couples argue and fight, as reconciliation that normally strengthen their bond usually follows arguments. Sure, Abby and I still have fights and disagreements, as do all couples, yet our golden rule is never to go to bed mad at each other. The key takeaway from this article was that "communication and laughter in your marriage are essential" (Sullivan 2021). While I will admit I am not the best communicator and an even worse listener, I try to keep things in my life a bit lighthearted with humor and laughter.

In the same anniversary interview with Abby, I asked about her thoughts on our life together. She said, "I feel very blessed to have found such a loving, supportive husband and life partner." I also wanted to know her thoughts on where we go from here. She eloquently replied, "It's one day at a time, as it's just two imperfect people refusing to give up on each other because of all the love and respect we have for one another."

One of the greatest tests of our marriage came during the summer of 2021 when we lived together for three months in a 240-square-foot tiny house in Elizabethtown, Pennsylvania. To add to the stress of tiny living, we were dealing with lots of life's curve balls thrown our way (e.g., my recent retirement after forty years of working, the second year of a worldwide pandemic, and a condominium renovation in Philadelphia that was taking much longer than anticipated and desired). Despite these challenges, we made the best of the difficult situation and enjoyed time reconnecting with friends and family in Pennsylvania.

In chess, the king and queen work closely together to protect the king from the opponent's attack. The queen is the most powerful chess piece on a chessboard, which is why it is so important to find a good partner who can work in tandem. In life, a husband and wife work together to protect each other from a variety of attacks, such as stress from careers as well as marital, financial, and other family issues.

As the Bible tells us in Proverbs 31:10 [CEV], "A truly good wife is the most precious treasure a man can find." Relationships are a challenging part of life, as it is difficult to find the special someone who is right for us. After many years of failed attempts, it came down to taking a friend's advice and finding a sweet, intelligent, and caring person who is still helping others today.

On June 13, 2022, we celebrated thirty-five years together, and I honestly feel Abby is the most precious gift in my life! The takeaway lesson is: *Take your time to find a good life partner to enhance your happiness.*

CHAPTER 3:

PERSEVERANCE PUSHES US TO ACHIEVE GOALS

———

Who has the perseverance these days to work for a company for almost twenty-five years?

In today's world, not many people stay at one company for over twenty years. I discovered the average American employee stays with their employer for only about four years (Kolmer 2022). What made me stay in Hershey for so long?

To fully appreciate the depth of my desire to work at HE&R for almost a quarter of a century, it is important to learn about how perseverance drove two men to do amazing philanthropic efforts that tie back to Hershey. In particular, let us learn more about Milton Hershey, a man who created what we know as Hershey today, and also about another young man, Kayvon Asemani, who benefited from Milton's vision as well as his greatest accomplishment.

There is probably no one in America who has not enjoyed a Hershey product of one kind or another. My favorite is the

Milk Chocolate with Almonds Bar. Milton Hershey founded the Hershey company at the turn of the twentieth century, but he was not always the successful philanthropist we think of today. The story of Hershey embodies the American dream of overcoming adversity, working hard, and building a life and a legacy. The man and the company have a fascinating story involving failed business ventures, bankruptcy, and a European inspiration that we all love.

According to the Hershey Community Archives, Milton Hershey failed twice before opening the Lancaster Caramel Company in 1886. Though the third try was the charm, even this company came close to completely failing. Bad credit plagued Hershey after previous failures in Philadelphia and New York City, and his caramel company was also in danger of failing. A bank cashier, Mr. Brenneman, at the Lancaster National Bank was very impressed with Milton's factory operation. Thus, he came to the rescue by cosigning the loan himself, giving Hershey the cash he needed for a batch of raw ingredients to keep the company going. It began to grow, and by 1892, he bought competitor's facilities as they made Hershey's caramels with the finest imported ingredients. His involvement in caramels was ultimately short-lived yet profitable, as he sold the caramel business in 1900 for one million dollars, equating to thirty-five million today. After seeing machines in Europe that made chocolate, Milton rethought his business plan and started making Hershey bars and changed candy history by making affordable chocolate available to everyone, much like Henry Ford did for automobiles.

Milton's greatest accomplishment occurred in 1909 when he and his wife, Catherine, who could not have children of their own, opened the Hershey Industrial School, a school and home for orphaned boys. Later renamed the Milton Hershey School, it serves over two thousand underprivileged boys and girls from across the United States. Milton's impact on the central Pennsylvania town of Hershey did not stop at the beautiful school campus.

After reading an intriguing article called "The Untold Truth of Hershey," I discovered Hershey's early struggles meant he understood what it was like to wonder where his next meal was coming from. When it came time to provide for his workers, he went to extremes. He started by designing and building Hershey, Pennsylvania, as not just a company town but as a place the workers in his factory would be proud to raise their families (Kelly 2021). It grew up in the earliest days of the chocolate factories and included not only nice houses but also affordable transportation, a park, an amusement park called Hersheypark today, a ballroom, a beautiful resort hotel called the Hotel Hershey today, and a swimming pool. When you visit Hershey, which I highly recommend, you can still see and visit many of the construction items built during the Great Depression of the 1930s. When you visit this town with its chocolate-kiss streetlights, you will be one of over six million visitors annually to "The Sweetest Place on Earth."

You must admit it is quite inspiring to hear about Milton Hershey's perseverance to follow his dreams despite numerous failures. It made me wonder why so many of us give up on our dreams. Tony Robbins, a bestselling author, speaker, and business strategist, explains that humans are imperfect beings, and we tend to give up on our dreams for all kinds of reasons (Robbins n.d.). There are several reasons for this: we get bored, fear failure, or "are not fortunate enough to be surrounded by supportive friends and family." As I discussed earlier, I was lucky to grow up in such a loving and supportive family. Robbins approaches roadblocks by suggesting you shift your mindset to turn obstacles into opportunities, discover your ultimate purpose in life, and connect every action to it. While it took me decades to realize it, my ultimate purpose is to teach others and increase their happiness. Lastly, in my opinion, the third and most important approach is to celebrate all successes and practice gratitude.

Learning about the amazing history of Hershey and what one man did for this community as a philanthropist inspired me to work even harder in my roles at HE&R for twenty-three years. Since the profitability of our company dictated how much of a dividend we paid to support the Milton Hershey School, it drove me to do whatever I could to help these amazing kids. Activities would include interactions with the students in various school settings (e.g., career fairs, dinners, community events) or doing something fun, like taking them to a Hershey Bears hockey game in our indoor arena.

Let me share a story about my chance meeting with a young man with whom I am lucky to be friends today. Kayvon Asemani is one of the many amazing graduates from the Milton Hershey School whom I met back in 2012 when he was only a sophomore in high school. While working at HE&R, I volunteered to speak about my profession, finance and accounting, to a group of high school students at the school's Career Day. While not the glitziest of professions, I remember one student in particular who was wide-eyed and glued to my every word, as he loved hearing about how the finance and accounting department was one of the most integral parts of any successful organization, at least, in my biased opinion. This same student had lots of great thought-provoking questions after my talk about how he could get more involved at HE&R. This student was Kayvon, who we hired as one of our brightest and most personable interns.

Today, Kayvon works at Meta Platforms as a product manager and is a musical artist in his spare time. Kayvon stays busy as a teacher for the Financial Literacy Community Project and student leader of the PennCORP Pre-Orientation Program, where he leads discussions about social issues and how we can increase our awareness to optimize impact.

I listened to an impactful TEDx Talk by Kayvon where he explains that despite growing up as an orphan, he has still reached success, and he has lived his life to show the world that people who come from less deserve a chance (Asemani 2018). In this talk, he tells his gripping story and shares his view on the importance of reaching happiness through achieving mental clarity. He says, in his freshman year at the University of Pennsylvania, "I was clinically depressed because the background I was coming from just really did not fit in with what was going on at Penn." Kayvon struggled academically—a new and unsettling experience for a straight-A high school student—and at one point thought seriously of transferring elsewhere. Kayvon further shared, "I was only five feet tall when I got to high school. I'm short now, but I was really short then, and I was getting bullied left and right because I was a nerd." He goes back a bit further when he shares, "In elementary school, that's when my father tried to murder my mother!"

Kayvon overcame obstacles most of us could never imagine. Kayvon was nine years old in 2005 when his father attempted to murder his mother in the family's Ellicott City, Maryland, apartment. The attack left his mother profoundly brain-damaged and permanently institutionalized, sent his father back to prison for thirty years, and essentially orphaned their three children. After graduating from high school at Milton Hershey in 2014, Kayvon received admission to the Wharton School of the University of Pennsylvania. While there, Kayvon taught financial literacy to West Philly kids, which deepened his commitment to social justice, while the playful, positive vibe of his music and videos helped make him a campus celebrity. He also landed a featured performance spot during the 2016 International Young Leaders Assembly at the United Nations (Rierdon 2021).

While Kayvon is a young man with a larger-than-life personality and a multi-megawatt smile, he appeared in *Forbes* magazine as one of the Most Outstanding Business School Grads of 2018. He became friends with author and Wharton professor Adam Grant, who introduced him to the former COO of Facebook, now Meta Platforms. After meeting him, Sheryl Sandberg hired him out of college. Kayvon sums it up best in the *Inquirer* article as follows: "My mother would be proud not only of me but of my siblings. We carried forward as we didn't throw it all away. I think our mother would be really proud of the fact that it wasn't all a waste. She has been here with us all along."

In his TEDx Talk, Kayvon talks about how you have to work on your own game and not be restricted by everyone else's expectations as follows, "That taught me a powerful lesson: as I wanted less for myself, I became happier." His challenging childhood drives him as follows: "I wanted to help create a world where other kids who come from broken homes have the opportunity to succeed just like I did, and that's the path I wanted to choose." In this must-listen TEDx Talk, Kayvon, just twenty-two at the time, discusses a focus of my book... happiness. He indicates that regardless of the good, the bad, or anything in between that happens to us and regardless of whose fault it is, it cannot impact our happiness.

So, after such a horrific childhood for him and his siblings, how did Kayvon feel about getting sent to Hershey for schooling? I spoke with Kayvon one-on-one to hear more about his personal journey since we crossed paths over a decade ago. He explained the meaning of going to the Milton Hershey School as follows: "I was born into welfare, so it has always been tough, but my mom taught me to look for opportunity in every situation." That worked out for Kayvon and his siblings when they received admission into the prestigious Milton Hershey School. He says, "We basically took that opportunity as our lifeline because we knew how lucky we were to get into such a well-endowed institution."

After meeting Kayvon in 2012, we hired him for two summer internships. He also was a summer intern for our owner, the Hershey Trust Company, after his freshman year at Wharton. In the same interview, Kayvon explained the importance of internships at the Hershey entities to his career as follows: "You understand the different dynamics between people. You understand the differences between an academic setting like school and a professional setting like work. There are many different things I learned as far as how to carry myself, how to communicate, how to make eye contact, how to be more concise, and communication." Just hearing Kayvon made me proud to have met such a dynamic life changing young man, and I still have him as a friend today.

In a *Forbes* article, the author says, "None of us get to where we are in life without some level of grit and perseverance" (Juetton 2020). I agree that while our intellect and ambition may assist us in taking on life's obstacles and challenges, perseverance is the quality that gets less than its due in our documentation of success stories. Milton Hershey failed miserably twice before he started making chocolate bars and changed the world of education. Kayvon grew up as an orphan under welfare and has become highly successful in his career as well as his philanthropic efforts. As the *Forbes* article sums up nicely, "We need that persistence, that perseverance, to allow us to achieve those goals in the face of obstacles that would otherwise derail us."

Perseverance is very important to crossing the finish line of a three-hour marathon or winning a grueling game of chess. I have competed in numerous lengthy chess matches. I learned it truly takes a well-prepared mental and physical body to endure the many permutations and attacks your opponent will throw at you during a tough chess match. Perseverance is truly a key element necessary for all of us to achieve our goals.

Why do I share these fascinating stories of Milton Hershey and Kayvon Asemani? Because they symbolize the importance of perseverance in life as both men got knocked down several times, picked themselves up, and made a lasting impact on the lives of others. This is the main reason why I worked at HE&R for almost a quarter of a century, as its primary mission was to support the Milton Hershey School that Milton had created in 1909. It allowed me to interact with amazing students, such as Kayvon, and the same well-renowned school that helped develop Kayvon into the outstanding young man he is today. Keep in mind our key lesson is: *Work for a company that means more than just a paycheck.*

CHAPTER 4:

CAREER CHALLENGES

———

Twenty percent of Americans have changed careers since the pandemic began in March 2020.

This intriguing statement comes from a Prudential survey of 2,000 Americans (Caporal 2022). It indicates that one out of every five of your friends, relatives, and acquaintances have changed jobs over the past two years of 2020 to 2021. This made me think about my career, which began with many job changes until I found a job I both enjoyed and fit nicely with my overall values.

According to a career advice article, only 54 percent of workers think their employer or leadership team is loyal to them, leading to a greater propensity to leave their jobs (Doyle 2020). Numerous reasons inspire us to depart our jobs, such as improved pay, benefits, and work-life balance. The article shares an interesting one for me: better alignment between personal values and organizational priorities. I feel this is a very important factor in the overall happiness and fulfillment in our jobs and, more importantly, in our lives.

Let's walk down memory lane to see how my career finally led me to better alignment, fulfillment, and happiness.

After graduating with honors from Gettysburg College in June 1981 with a bachelor of arts degree specializing in accounting, I completed a short one-year stint in public accounting in Harrisburg, Pennsylvania. After passing the challenging certified public accountant (CPA) exam, I furthered my career in 1982 as a financial analyst at Harrisburg Steel Company (HARSCO) in Camp Hill, where my introduction into the corporate world involved finding my desk in a storage area on my first day. In 1984, I transferred to their defense division, Bowen-McLaughlin-York (BMY) in York, where I worked for the next six years. BMY, now known as BAE Systems, is a defense contractor that makes tanks and other fighting vehicles for US and international customers. During my time at BMY, I met two life-impacting people: Abby Warner, my wonderful wife and life partner for over thirty-five years, and Bryan Stambaugh, my best friend.

As with many people, I bounced around with four different jobs during the early stages of my career. The first ten years of my career were typical for many Americans. I was actively looking for work throughout my first decade as I hadn't found *the right job* yet. Upon research, I discovered that the average American employee holds twelve jobs throughout their lifetime. The article also states that almost two-thirds, 65 percent, of American workers are actively searching for a new full-time job as of January 2022 (Kolmer 2022).

The average person spends over 90,000 hours at work throughout their lifetime, or one-third of their lives working (Vaughn 2018). Since we spend a large portion of our lives working, I felt it imperative to find a job that was both fulfilling and served a greater mission than just making the shareholders happy. This can be very challenging as, in most cases, we are just happy to find a job that pays the bills despite being senselessly boring.

Shockingly, I discovered that with an ever-increasing number of career choices, 30 percent of the workforce will now change careers or jobs every twelve months (DOL n.d.). If people are changing jobs so often, it made me wonder what the most common reasons for a career change are. As the article indicates, several common reasons are the ones we would expect, such as more money, frustration with the job or your boss, and hating the company culture. A surprising one that resonated with me was a realignment of personal or spiritual values.

After ten years of drifting between jobs, my big career break came when I started working at my fifth job of six during my career at HE&R, a world-class entertainment and hospitality company. My new role began in January 1991 as managing director of finance of the Sports and Entertainment Group, which included their largest division, Hersheypark. As we learned in an earlier chapter, Milton Hershey created Hersheypark as a leisure ground for Hershey's Chocolate Factory employees. If you have not visited this beautiful fun-filled amusement park yet, stop reading now and make plans for you and your family to do so. According to a local newspaper, over three million people attend Hersheypark annually, making it one of North America's twenty most visited parks (Shannon 2017).

Over the next twenty-three years at HE&R, I worked with many influential mentors who shaped my career and made me a better person and a respected leader. After two years of long hours at the operating division level, I transferred over to the corporate world in 1993 for a better work-life balance and to return to the corporate office environment I was familiar with in my prior work at HARSCO. Unlike my prior HARSCO corporate stint, this time, a desk and an office with a window awaited me at the corporate offices located in beautiful Hershey, Pennsylvania.

My corporate career started with working for Scott Newkam, who was the chief financial officer (CFO) and vice president of finance at the time. When Scott was promoted to president and CEO, he navigated our company with calm leadership through some very challenging times. He also became a life-long mentor for me for the rest of my career. An interesting side note is Scott would text me every holiday to check on Abby and me until he passed away unexpectedly in May 2022. This special touch from a respected leader was a great lesson for me in leadership. Treat everyone with respect and stay in touch when possible, even if it is a brief message.

In my opinion, one of the keys to successful leadership is to have supportive and strong staff members. While there are too many folks to list, I certainly want to thank all the amazing staff members who helped me more than they will ever know. The highlight of my twenty-three-year career at HE&R was working for Bill Simpson, retired president and CEO, who is still a good friend and mentor today. I learned a lot about leadership from Bill. During some of the darkest days in my career, which we will hear about later in the book,

Bill always showed empathy and support for my finance team and me. My early retirement from HE&R and subsequent switch to academia raised some eyebrows from friends and family. Despite my values changing to educating others, Bill was extremely supportive of my teaching stint for the next seven years in Illinois. Even though I retired from Hershey over eight years ago in 2014, I still maintain contact with Bill, as he is truly a lifelong mentor to me. Thanks, Bill, for your guidance and leadership!

While there were several positives about my work, there were also many challenges. As discussed above, the most challenging concept in your career is when you consider a major career change after deciding to switch industries. Moving from the business world, where I had spent thirty-three years, to academia was a particularly difficult transition.

One of the challenges I faced as a professor was during my initial semester of teaching in the fall of 2014 at the University of Illinois at Urbana-Champaign (UIUC). The role of lecturer at the larger university level was very challenging for me while tasked with teaching three classes at the master's level for students not majoring in accounting. As with any new job, during the first several months I dedicated many hours outside of class preparing my lectures, creating challenging exams, and completing grading rubrics while holding office hours.

In October 2014, after teaching for only six weeks, I accepted an offer to teach an online accounting course as part of our university's offering of a fully online Master's in Business Administration (named the "iMBA") program. The university would offer this course on the worldwide Coursera education platform, which works with universities to offer online courses, certifications, and degrees in a variety of subjects. Developing an online course involved a considerable amount of work. The workload involved creating scripts for short lecture videos and taping these sessions in a recording studio.

Since I still had a bit of a stigma from not having a PhD and was anxious to prove myself as an effective teacher in this large university setting, I said yes to the online course offer. I created an introductory video and sat in lots of meetings with several world-renowned professors from our prestigious College of Business (COB). Many of these meetings included Coursera representatives as well as members from our amazing e-Learning team within the COB.

The first semester was incredibly challenging. I struggled to keep up with the many online course meetings and requirements in addition to my normal teaching load. After a much-needed Christmas holiday break, I had completed only two weeks of the required sixteen of online course offerings by the end of January 2015. After discussions with Abby, I realized I could not keep up with the demands of online course development in addition to my normal course teaching load.

In one of my more difficult meetings in my new world of academia, I met with my department chair, Jon Davis, on February 3, 2015, on a cold and dreary winter morning. As perspiration beaded on my forehead, I nervously explained to him that I was stressed and unable to complete the online course development. After expressing some disappointment, he very calmly indicated that he knew of another accounting professor who would be able to jump in and complete the online course. He would speak with Gary soon and let me know. I was extremely relieved when Jon emailed me later that night to let me know the good news. Gary went on to create an extremely popular and highly rated online managerial accounting course on the Coursera platform.

Agreeing to do things outside your job description can and does lead to burnout (Odogwu 2022). In my opinion, the real question when someone proposes additional work projects to you is to truly determine *if* you can deliver great results. For example, when I turned down the online Coursera teaching opportunity in 2015, I admitted to my boss it would not be a quality course as the University of Illinois expected. Thus, by saying no at times in your career, the article states you are on the right track and will earn you the respect of those who matter.

After a challenging start to my academic career, I wondered what other people I know and respect have experienced in their career changes. In a June 2022 interview with Brian Hamm, a clinical assistant professor at the University of Illinois, I was curious about what made him switch from being a C-Suite finance executive for the past twenty years to being an award-winning accounting professor. Brian stated the following: "It's something that I've always wanted to do. It was being able to share the experiences and the lessons learned and some of the mistakes I made throughout my career with students so that they can put it into practice and learn from my mistakes." Like me, Brian faced similar challenges in his career transition. Brian was CFO at Energizer and vice president of finance at Pepsi. Going from senior levels within large organizations to being a clinical assistant professor and switching jobs is a very humbling experience.

As we have discussed, while we all face obstacles in our career transitions, I wanted to know what Brian felt were the biggest rewards of his career switch. He quickly replied, "It's when the student, who had your class two to four semesters ago, reaches out and wants your advice." I did not think about this mentoring part of teaching until I experienced it with several students in my first several years at Illinois. The best reward was what Brian described next: "Just to send you the note that says, 'Hey, you made a difference in my life, man,' that's a darn good feeling." Lastly, I wanted to know if Brian had any advice for readers contemplating a career change. He offered, "Ask many questions and be vulnerable, as I found that people genuinely want to help, and they feel pride when they can help pass on some of the best practices." This is sage advice from an award-winning professor.

In my heyday of playing chess in high school, I would go to numerous weekend tournaments to challenge myself by playing with stronger opponents. Similar to my initial decade of employment, I would bounce around between various opening moves and playing styles. After many losses to more disciplined experienced players, I finally realized a defensive style of play suited my personality much better than an aggressive one. My perseverance in losing many games made me a much better chess player over time, as I truly loved winning games by patiently waiting for my opponent to make a mistake.

In summation, after numerous job changes over the initial decade of my career, I loved working at Hershey for twenty-three years. Our mission statement and core purpose provide value to the Milton Hershey School, which serves over two thousand underprivileged boys and girls from across the US. Working at Hershey was an amazing opportunity to work for a much higher purpose. Similar to the tasty chocolate aroma you smell as you drive through the streets of Hershey lined with kiss-shaped lights, what is not to love about working for such a philanthropic mission? As Michelle Obama said, "Success is not about how much money you make. It's about the difference you make in people's lives" (CNN 2020). The takeaway lesson is: *Find a job that has special meaning, even if it takes a long time!*

CHAPTER 5:

ACHIEVING CAREER GOALS!

Every one of us has career goals. What are yours?

As an avid (although not particularly good) tennis player, I love watching tennis matches on television. I witnessed one of the biggest upsets in September 2019 when Bianca Andreescu, a nineteen-year-old Canadian tennis player, upset highly ranked Serena Williams, the greatest women's tennis player of her generation. When asked how she thwarted the thirty-seven-year-old Williams's attempt to match the record of twenty-four major singles titles, she indicated that for years she had closed her eyes and envisioned herself winning the United States Open against Serena Williams. According to a *New York Times* article, Andreescu said, "For it to become a reality is so crazy," breaking down in tears in her post-match news conference. "I guess these visualizations really, really work" (Clarey 2019).

According to a *Forbes* article, there are three powerful ways successful people achieve their most ambitious career goals.

Those are: visualize success; focus on the process, not the outcome; and write down your goals while dreaming big. Psychology professor Dr. Gail Matthews at the Dominican University in California led a study on goal-setting with nearly 270 participants. She found that participants were 42 percent more likely to achieve their goals just by writing them down (Castrillon 2020).

Like Bianca, I had career goals. I had always dreamed of being the top financial executive in a company and visualized how I would treat my staff with respect and compassion. I had no idea it would come to fruition in such an odd manner. In the fall of 2010, I was incredibly happy as controller and budget director of HE&R when my boss, Dave Lavery, the chief financial officer (CFO) and vice president of finance, called me into his office to discuss an important issue. At the time, I was in a great role. I enjoyed being the number two person in the HE&R corporate finance department and working with such a dedicated, hard-working staff. At fifty-one, I was only nine years away from my goal of retiring at age sixty.

As happens to many of us in our careers, things can change quickly. Dave explained the offer he received to be the interim chief executive officer (CEO) of our parent company, the Hershey Trust Company, which was a tremendous opportunity for him. His interim CEO role would last until the Trust had found a permanent CEO. In his absence, he and the executive committee, a group of eight senior executives, had agreed that I was the best internal candidate to fill his shoes as interim CFO if I wanted to accept the position. While I was excited they would assign me this significant role, it made me quite nervous. The company was navigating some challenging times, including divestitures of several divisions. I knew it would require much arduous work, and I was already quite busy in my current role. It was decision time. I remember vividly going to the restroom after the job offer from Dave and thinking, *What the hell just happened?*

After discussing the interim CFO role and increased responsibilities with Abby, I decided to step out of my comfort zone and take the position with the understanding it would be a short-term assignment of one year or so until Dave returned. The next eighteen months were the most challenging of my twenty-three-year career at HE&R. I became extremely busy and stressed. To compound the situation, the company experienced an incredibly challenging year in 2011.

I am sure you have heard the phrase "bad things come in threes," which I had never really believed until 2011. Our company, which derived almost 60 percent of its revenue from the summer months of Memorial Day to Labor Day, was hit with the following three events over five to six months, as follows:

1) A very rainy weather pattern throughout our critical summer season severely impacted attendance at Hersheypark, our outdoor amusement park. This led to huge revenue shortfalls to our budgeted targets by midyear, thus forcing us to go into numerous cost-cutting or contingency efforts directed by our finance department under my guidance.

2) In September, Tropical Storm Lee provided over twelve inches of rainfall from September fifth through the eighth,

which caused significant flooding throughout our Hershey properties, including our main source of revenue, Hersheypark. Per the National Weather Service, heavy rain from the remnants of Tropical Storm Lee led to historic flooding in the mid-Atlantic region, especially Central Pennsylvania. Total estimated damage costs from Tropical Storm Lee exceeded two billion dollars (Grumm 2011). This weather event further exasperated our 2011 budget shortfalls.

3) In October, Hersheypark's general manager and a close personal friend of mine, Frank O'Connell, passed away at age forty-eight.

This series of challenging times required me to become a different type of leader.

By listening to a leadership expert's TEDx Talk, I learned leadership requires communicating with transparency as well as sharing information as often as possible. Leaders must share what they know and admit what they do not. During these stressful times, humility is important (Edmondson 2020).

Paradoxically, honesty creates more psychological safety for others. It is far more important to communicate when you do not have all the answers than when you do. As I learned from my boss at the time, Bill Simpson, we needed to keep the entire company in the loop as to the financial struggles we were facing in 2011. We accomplished this goal through operational town hall meetings where, as interim CFO, I would share the dismal financial reports, and together we would work to cut discretionary costs to help offset our top-line revenue shortfalls.

Edmondson's TEDx Talk also taught me to act with urgency despite incomplete information. Admitting you do not have the answers does not mean avoiding action, as inaction leaves people feeling lost and very unstable. During our HE&R management meetings as well as town hall meetings with all employees, we communicated we did not have all the answers. We did have a plan in place. The summer and fall seasons of 2011 presented a very fluid environment, and we tried to manage as urgently as possible. The key takeaway from this informative TEDx Talk was that one of the most effective ways to show leadership is to share power with those around you. While our instincts are to hold even more tightly to control in times of upheaval, it usually backfires. This was a particularly valuable lesson for me during my interim CFO role, as Bill Simpson taught me a critical senior leadership lesson. Give your managers the proper training and tools to lead their staff members, and then, "Get out of their way and let them lead."

Despite all the trials and tribulations during my eighteen-month role as interim CFO, I learned the valuable lesson that, occasionally, you have to step outside your comfort zone to become a stronger person. Thanks to my mentor, Bill Simpson, and my dedicated staff, I learned to become a better leader and take on future challenges with a clearer mind. This painful lesson learned over the difficult period of October 2010 through March 2012 was immensely helpful for me when I encountered challenges in my later career as a professor and, more recently, as an author.

After some research on setting goals and measuring progress, I found a great article on setting a SMART goal, which is an acronym that stands for specific, measurable, achievable, realistic, and time-bound (Martins 2022). Let's discuss each concept briefly, with examples:

Specific: Ensure you are setting a specific goal. (You want to save $3,000 for a 2025 summer vacation to Paris.)

Measurable: Your goal should be measurable objectively. (You need to save $300 every month over the next ten months.)

Achievable: While your goal should not be easy to achieve, this concept indicates it should not be outside the realm of possibility. (You want to learn French for your upcoming trip to Paris. While you cannot be fluent in a few months, your goal of learning from a foreign language application for twenty to thirty minutes a day is more achievable.)

Realistic: Similar to the above concept, the goal should also be realistic. (Setting a goal to practice speaking French for two hours per day is not realistic. The above goal of twenty to thirty minutes of practicing French is much more realistic.)

Time-bound: Your goal should have an end date or deadline. (You need to complete the savings and language goals by July 1, 2025.)

Hopefully, you will find the value you get from setting SMART goals will outweigh the additional time spent on this thought-provoking goal-setting process.

Reflecting on my second goal of becoming a professor with a significant impact on my students, I realize I experienced many highs and lows in academia. As described in the prior chapter, my failure to teach the online distance learning class in January 2015 was the low point of my academic career. Fortunately, there were many positive highlights. I was fortunate to receive the Department Chair Award for Excellence in Accountancy Education for the academic year 2015 to 2016. Despite my prior failure in the growing e-learning environment, the department head, Jon Davis, with whom I had failed before, chose me in the fall of 2016 to create an online version of my successful intermediate accounting course for our university's offering of the first fully distance education masters of science in accounting degree (named the iMSA program) in the country. This time, I was much better prepared to handle the e-learning course development demands, since I had two years of teaching under my belt and the online support team at our College of Business had grown as well.

During the next nine months of development, I worked closely with the amazing Illinois online development staff to expand materials for building a massive open online course (MOOC), which is an online course aimed at unlimited participation and open access via the web. My two eight-week courses were some of the initial online accounting courses from the University of Illinois before COVID-19 made online courses hip. They placed my courses on the worldwide Coursera educational platform during the summer of 2017. I learned a lot, as writing detailed scripts for my online videos made me a better teacher in the classroom with my live students as well.

While I learned having competent reliable staff at Hershey was critical to my career success, I found having a great assistant was equally important during the development and rollout of a successful online course. During this course development process, I met one of my favorite students, Zack Smith, who was my online teaching assistant (TA) for the next two years of my online master's-level courses. Zack was instrumental in the success of my courses as he developed hundreds of challenging accounting questions for the Coursera online students. He also sat next to me from 2016 to 2017 in the Business Instructional Facility (BIF) production studio for the initial offerings of my iMSA course. Zack became much more than a TA. He is a friend and has joined Abby and me for dinner. Zack has also attended various athletic events with us at the university. In addition to Zack, I met some amazing online students who have gone on to become CPAs, CFOs, and even professors.

My fondest memories of the worldwide impact of my teaching include the fact there have been over 250,000 visitors to my Coursera course websites from 130 countries as of November 2022. There have been over 43,000 learners in my two online courses, and 6,000 students have completed my courses for an online completion rate of 14 percent. According to a United Kingdom Study, completion rates (defined as the percentage of enrolled students who completed the course) for online courses vary widely from 1 percent to 52 percent, with a median value of 12.6 percent (Jordan 2015). My two courses, Accounting Analysis I: The Role of Accounting as an Information System, and its follow-up course, Accounting Analysis I: Measurement and Disclosure of Assets, both have a stellar rating of 4.8 out of five stars.

The best measure of the success of an online course comes from student reviews and comments. In particular, I enjoyed a recent review from a student, Yuliya, from Ukraine, who found my course to be very informative and useful in his attempt to build a new life. This has even more meaning since Russia's February 2022 invasion of Ukraine. I also received the Excellence-in-Teaching Award in May 2019 for extraordinary commitment and dedication to students in the iMSA program, which was very meaningful because my online students voted.

There is no greater feeling of accomplishment than taking on an additional work assignment and knocking it out of the park. My increased experience and confidence in my teaching abilities made me much better prepared for the 2016 Coursera online opportunity, which led to phenomenal results. After such a difficult start to my college teaching career, the lessons I learned from these experiences are that you need to step outside your comfort zone to achieve your career goals. Also, when challenges present themselves, every so often, you must say *no* if the project is outside of your job description or you are simply unprepared for this type of effort.

As a competitive chess player in high school, I remember several matches against much stronger opponents where I thought I would certainly lose the match. Even though my opponent would exert lots of pressure on my king in the first twenty moves of the game, I would somehow develop a plan of attack during the middle part of the game that would enable me to turn the tables. While the game of chess does not match the rigors of life, I learned at an early age to step outside of my comfort zone to achieve my goal of helping my chess team win the overall match.

Stepping outside my comfort zone has led to the success and achievement of several of my career goals, such as serving as CFO of a major company and becoming a professor with a substantial impact on my students. In addition, I had dreamed of becoming an author and writing a book to help others achieve some measure of happiness similar to what I have experienced in my life. Let me share a brief story of how my retirement goal of becoming an author came to fruition.

Newly retired, I caught up with Bill Simpson over lunch at the Hershey Country Club during the summer of 2021. He shared that he enjoyed retirement and found ways to stay busy during the pandemic from 2020 to 2021. I owe him a debt of gratitude, as he introduced me to Eric Koester and the Georgetown University Book Creators community-based author program. I had dreamed of writing a book as an end-of-career goal. In my initial discussion with Eric in December 2021, he shared several positives that can come from writing a book: It forced folks to reflect on their lives, and the other was the sense of accomplishment. I could not agree more with both of these, as it has been challenging, frustrating, enjoyable, and incredibly humbling during my fourteen-month journey.

Achieving career goals is demanding work. Occasionally you need to step outside your comfort zones, when appropriate, to be successful. I would like to close this chapter with a quick story on how Bill has impacted my career goals as he has mentored me throughout the various phases of my life.

When he agreed to be a beta reader to provide early feedback on my manuscript, I was excited as I knew Bill would provide honest and reliable input since he has read numerous leadership and career enhancement books. On a day when I was feeling down after receiving a fair amount of negative feedback from several other editors and beta readers, it was extremely comforting and reassuring to hear from Bill that "he was enjoying my book." Our chapter lesson is: *Stepping outside your comfort zone to achieve career goals is hard yet rewarding, and it is okay to say no.*

CHAPTER 6:

CHANGING CAREERS IS EASY... RIGHT?

It took a worldwide pandemic for many of us to realize how much we hated our jobs and careers.

According to a CNBC article, a report found a whopping 93 percent of Americans said they are not currently pursuing their dream career (Dickler 2021). It turns out very few Americans are happy with their current position or job. The report found that as many as 95 percent of workers would consider a job change, and 92 percent are even willing to switch industries to find the right position.

In addition to my work at Hershey, I taught at local colleges as an adjunct instructor from 1999 through 2011 and enjoyed interacting with students in a classroom setting. As I explained, the last several years at Hershey were incredibly stressful in the temporary eighteen-month role of interim CFO at HE&R. I realized my happiest days at work were the same days I was teaching my evening classes at local colleges. I enjoyed being in front of a class and sharing my past experiences in the business world to show my students how to apply various accounting and finance topics to real-world scenarios.

After numerous sleepless nights and various discussions with Abby on whether we should fulfill our goals as discussed, I decided to change careers and move into academia full time. With the full support of Abby, I overcame my fear of the unknown as the sixth and final job during my career of four decades was the hardest to garner.

In an interview with Michael Peterson, an award-winning business professor at McCombs School of Business at the University of Texas at Austin, I learned he always loved teaching and being in front of people. "Working with super-sharp colleagues and bright, hard-working students adds up to a dream job." In my interview, I discovered his road to academia was shorter than mine, as he was already serving as a guest lecturer. Michael said, "I simply received a call from a former professor about a teaching role at his alma mater." Michael is drafting an upcoming book, *From Business Professional to Business Professor,* which will cover many of these transition aspects (Peterson 2023). In this chapter, we will discover how making a career change is not easy, but it is usually worthwhile in the long run.

As my boss at HE&R, Dave Lavery, was about to announce my early retirement in June 2013, I discovered I had no idea of how difficult it would be to switch careers, especially when it meant trying to obtain a full-time teaching position in academia. After numerous failures to obtain an interview with colleges in my local area, I decided to expand my search outside of the Pennsylvania area. I made this decision jointly with Abby because it meant we would have to relocate to another part of the country, and she would have to leave her role as a pathologist at York Hospital. She loved her coworkers and developed strong ties to her pathology group after working there from 2000 through 2013. We agreed to move into an early retirement phase to spend more time together and do things we felt were more useful to others, such as teaching and philanthropy.

My dismal job search made for a very disappointing summer until I decided to attend the American Accounting Association Annual Meeting in Anaheim, California, in August 2013. This huge convention of over 2,500 accounting professionals in academia also offered a job fair, where I met the folks from the University of Illinois at Urbana-Champaign (UIUC). After some hiccups in traveling out to the West Coast, the interview went well, and they invited Abby and me to visit their campus in October. I am a firm believer everything happens for a reason. I felt relieved after my exhaustive day-long interview process when I realized I was interviewing in a campus building on *Gregory* Drive and meeting with the accounting department chair, Jon *Davis*. The stars nicely aligned as I received the job offer a few weeks later to start my teaching role at the start of their next academic year in August 2014. I was excited to be a lecturer of accountancy at one of the top-ranked accounting schools in the country.

At the recommendation of the UIUC department chair, I attended an intense Association to Advance Collegiate Schools of Business (AACSB) Bridge Program at Georgetown University in June 2014, which helps executives transition into academic roles. The week-long Bridge Program does exactly what the name implies. It helps business professionals bridge from the boardroom to the classroom. Quite simply, I wanted to become an excellent—not just mediocre—professor at the university level. Attending this bridge program was a terrific way to learn the necessary tools to succeed. Excellent instructors dedicated to helping you launch your teaching career are part of the program's organization. I strongly recommend this program to anyone interested in changing careers and hoping to teach at the college level. The award-winning Michael Peterson attended this same conference a few years later.

While reading an article on why people fail at switching jobs, I learned several valuable lessons: choosing a new career path should be done with care, and spending time with people who perform the work you want to do is vital, along with extensive research (O'Donnell 2018). As I reflect on my career change in 2013, I did not do enough research or spend time with full-time faculty to understand the importance of having a PhD in academia. The article goes on to state, "In the end, successful career changers will tell you they never gave up, and they gave it all they had. You have got to be prepared for rejection and failure and still keep going." While I felt rejected and experienced many failures during the summer of 2013, I persevered and became successful in my new field.

After taking early retirement at age fifty-four from HE&R in January 2014, we moved away from friends and family to Champaign, Illinois, six months later. I embarked on the most rewarding seven years of my forty-year career by teaching various accounting courses at the prestigious University of Illinois at Urbana-Champaign. It served as my way of giving back to the accounting profession, as I loved interacting and sharing my experiences with the intelligent, energetic Illinois students (a.k.a. "the Fighting Illini").

One of my favorite students was a bright young lady, Kishyori (Kiyo) Kamaludin, who would arrive promptly for my 8:00 a.m. class with an engaging smile. In all my years of teaching, she is the only student to have achieved perfect scores on all the challenging quizzes in my difficult intermediate accounting classes. As of September 2022, she works as an assurance staff member at the international accounting and consulting firm CDH. Her recommendation of me on my LinkedIn site indicates, "Professor Gregory Davis is an outstanding instructor and a passionate individual. He loves teaching, and that translates very clearly to the students. He was my ACCY301 professor in the fall of 2019, and I had a brilliant experience as a student in his course."

As mentioned earlier in this chapter, in my interview with Michael Peterson, he indicated, "I love everything that's about being in front of my students. It is so much fun to be with them, ask and answer their questions, and see the lights go on. I love seeing them have success." One of my favorite activities at the University of Illinois was holding "coffee chats" in a casual one-on-one discussion with my students. Over coffee or tea, my simple rule was we could discuss anything other than accounting concepts, which we covered during our three hours of classroom time each week. The students loved hearing my war stories as well as things I have learned from my past experiences. In fact, after a second coffee chat where we discussed his career goals, one of my students told me I should write a book. As I am drafting this book years later, it is the best advice I have ever received from a student.

An article discussing why career changes are so challenging states the Holmes-Rahe Life Stress Inventory puts changing careers as one of the most twenty stressful things that happen in your life (Berger 2019). It is right behind the death of a close friend, which I have experienced as well. I would agree, as many things ran through my mind when I was contemplating a career change to academia: Could we manage a lifestyle change with a much lower salary, would I enjoy teaching every day, and would I regret leaving my stable job in Hershey? The article discusses a key theme of this book: "The quest for happiness is all around us. It is important to find a job that gives you a sense of purpose and fulfillment." While challenging, teaching made me happy and gave me an amazing sense of fulfillment.

Since I was new to academia, it was not an easy transition. Administrative assistants and staff did many things for me as an executive in the business world. I had no idea how much they spoiled me. Thanks to Kari, my office neighbor and friend, I navigated my office building and classrooms more efficiently. Despite the long distance, we remain friends today almost nine years later. I spent much time developing my class slides, lecture notes, and grading rubrics for my various assignments. As I quickly learned, a grading rubric is a scoring tool that explicitly represents the performance expectations for any assignment. Even though I was working long days in academia, I was loving life as I thoroughly enjoyed interacting with my students, and my work-life balance improved dramatically. I held my classes on Mondays and Wednesdays, typically from the dreaded 8:00 a.m. class to the early afternoon, and then I would hold office hours after my classes. I enjoyed my teaching lifestyle, as it freed up lots of time to spend with Abby.

Choose a job that you love and you won't have to work another day.

— *CONFUCIUS*

I pulled this quote from an interesting website dedicated to empowering young people to be active, civil, and curious citizens (Dixon 2015). On this website, a young lady, Claire Kittle Dixon, says, "I remember hearing people say this when I was just embarking on life after college. To be frank, I thought it was a bunch of malarkey." This quote sounds a bit cheesy (sorry, Confucius), and I did not believe this concept for many years of my young career. If this were true, someone would be paying me millions of dollars to play baseball, which is one of my favorite passions. Claire says, "But after an unfulfilling stint in the private sector, I got into the liberty movement and haven't looked back. Believe it or not, the quote is true." As I discovered in my difficult career change to academia, Confucius was right.

Some folks were curious why I enjoyed the weird game of chess. They marveled how I could sit and play an exhausting three-hour chess match inside a building while other fellow high school students were enjoying outdoor activities. Quite simply, I loved playing chess. I was happily playing this complicated game that made the challenges of learning chess worth the effort.

Despite the lack of a PhD and no prior full-time teaching experience, I was highly successful in my new career field. During my interview for the UIUC teaching job, I asked my boss, Jon Davis, how important it was for him to see accountancy professors on a list compiled each semester by the University of Illinois, which reflects student ratings of instruction called the "List of Teachers Ranked as Excellent by Their Students." Jon replied that it was very important and that we do not have enough accountancy professors on this list. I was determined to work hard, as it was my goal for my students to name me to this List of Excellent Teachers at some point in my teaching career at Illinois. I would have been happy being named just one semester to this lofty list.

Through a heavy time commitment as well as assistance from my excellent graduate teaching assistants (thanks Jay, Brian, Emily, Cathy, and others) and other world-class professors, I am honored to say I was named to the List of Excellent Teachers for all fourteen semesters of my UIUC teaching career. The lesson here is: *A career change is hard work, yet finding a job you love is worth the effort!*

CHAPTER 7:

PERSONAL FINANCE TIPS

Do you remember the rush that pulsed through your entire body when you opened your first paycheck?

I was excited to open my first monthly paycheck after graduating from Gettysburg College in June 1981. My annual salary was a whopping $15,000, so my simple math indicated it would be a check for almost $1,250. When I opened my check, the amount of only about $750 shocked me. What happened to my hard-earned money?

Fast forward to thirty-five years later, and my Illinois students discovered something similar. I was enjoying a coffee chat with one of my accounting students in the fall of 2016 when he asked me how much I made as a starting salary out of college. When I told him only $15,000, he laughed and wondered how I survived on such a meager amount. Then I asked how much he thought he would make after his five years of college, including a master's degree, and he said he hoped to make four times my starting salary, or $60,000.

Then he went on to say he figured a net monthly check of around $5,000 would be enough to afford a nice apartment in Chicago as well as a car and several vacations each year to various ski resorts. He was shocked and upset when I told him he would be lucky to take home $3,000, or only 60 percent, of his gross salary.

Since very few of us, if any, have had formal training, it is clear we all need a primer on the facets of personal finance. Michigan became the fourteenth state to mandate a personal finance course in high school (Tumulty 2022). The article states that personal finance should be as core to high school education as Shakespeare and algebra. I could not agree more, as I am fairly sure I use budgets and savings terms more on a daily basis than equations, variables, or citing famous Shakespeare phrases.

After reading a finance article, I learned that our gross income, $15,000 in my example above, is quite different from our net income or take-home pay (Consumer Finance 2022). We will have numerous payroll deductions, some we can impact while others are required by various government agencies, as follows:

1. Payroll taxes: The payroll taxes taken from your paycheck include Social Security and Medicare taxes, also called FICA (Federal Insurance Contributions Act) taxes. The Social Security tax provides retirement and disability benefits for employees and their dependents. The Medicare tax provides medical benefits to people aged 65 or older.

2. Income taxes: The government will determine how much you owe based on the amount of money you receive from earned income (salaries, wages, tips, and commissions) and unearned income (interest and dividends). As the name implies, federal income tax rates are the same across the country. In addition, some states and localities also have state and local income taxes.
3. Other deductions: These include pretax deductions, which include contributions to retirement accounts (e.g., 401[k] and 403[b] accounts) in addition to health care or medical plan coverage costs.

Let's review how much each of these payroll deductions costs you using the state of Pennsylvania as an example:

- Payroll taxes = 7.65 percent up to a maximum salary base of $160,200 in 2023 (SSA n.d.).
- Income taxes = approximately 19 percent (assumes federal of 15 percent, state of 3 percent, and local of 1 percent).
- Other = 13 percent (assumes average medical employee cost of 7 percent and 401(k) retirement cost of 6 percent).

The total cost of these deductions adds up to almost 40 percent of your paycheck.

The above example is per my final HE&R pay stub.

In summary, my coffee chat back in 2016 made me aware we need to understand our paychecks better to curtail our current spending and maximize our future retirement savings through Social Security and company 401(k)/403(b) plans. Now that we understand the details of how much our pay is, let us now turn our attention to the use of budgets to determine how to manage our spending and better prepare for our retirement years. President Barack Obama summarized a budget as follows: "A budget is more than just a series of numbers on a page; it is an embodiment of our values" (Obama Speeches 2005).

I listened to a TEDx Talk by Wendy De La Rosa, a Wharton assistant professor and cocreator and host of the TED series "Your Money and Your Mind." In her TEDx Talk, I learned it may make sense to take a "Financial Health Day to get your financial life in order" (De La Rosa 2021). To be successful, you need to commit to this day and make it as productive as possible. The first step is to focus on your fixed expenses, and you can best achieve this by using a term most people hate: budgets.

We have discussed the impact of taxes and deductions on our net pay. The real question is, what do budgets have to do with retirement? As budget director for Hershey for over ten years, I learned annual budgets are a critical component of any long-range strategic plan. While at Hershey, we created and reviewed five-year operational plans, which helped guide our annual budgeting process. Thus, I decided years ago using budgets would be extremely helpful in keeping Abby and me on a steady path to a happy retirement.

To make budgeting easier for my wife and me, we have used software called You Need a Budget (YNAB) for the past ten years. This software can be accessed online via YouNeed-aBudget.com and also offers an app for your cell phone, which allows you to quickly enter a transaction and see how much money is remaining in any expense category. YNAB breaks our monthly budget into four main categories of spending as follows:

- Immediate obligations (mortgage, utilities, groceries);
- True expenses (auto maintenance and gas, medical expenses, clothing);
- Quality of life goals (vacation, fitness); and
- Just for fun (dining out, sporting events).

I learned from Wendy's TEDx Talk that it is also "very important to create a savings goal or plan including an emergency reserve of three to six months, and the best way to achieve this goal is to set up automatic savings from a paycheck." One of the most popular methods of developing a sound budget is building it around a simple financial principle: pay yourself first.

After reading a great article, I discovered, "Paying yourself first is considered the golden rule by financial planners as you set aside the amount you have committed to saving before doing anything else with the rest of your paycheck" (Levitt 2022). The easiest way to achieve this is to open a savings account, if you do not already have one, at the bank where you maintain a checking account. Be sure to make it an automatic transfer from your paycheck, either for each payday or once a month. If you have access to an employer-sponsored retirement plan, such as a 401(k), contribute to that type of plan first before contributing to a savings account. Your money will accumulate tax-free (sorry, IRS), and many employers will match your contribution. We will discuss 401(k) plans further in a later chapter.

To achieve this basic principle, review your spending over the past three to four months and determine your average spending by expense category. You can make this process much easier by using your budget software or app (e.g., YNAB), since their reports are useful in tracking your spending habits. Once you calculate the average amount you know you are spending every month, you will be able to determine how much you can afford to save.

Experts recommend you should aim to save 10 to 15 percent of your pretax income to enhance your retirement funds (O'Shea 2022). This targeted annual savings goal includes any employer match from your company 401(k) plan. If this does not seem achievable, I recommend you should save a minimum of 5 percent with the intent to increase your savings on an annual basis (e.g., with annual pay raises and promotions) until you can meet the above 10 to 15 percent recommended guideline.

Wendy also emphasized in her TEDx Talk that it is important to talk to your significant other about money and ensure both of you are on the same page. Let us learn how Abby and I have accomplished this goal, as many couples argue and struggle in dealing with financial issues. A study revealed almost half (48 percent) of US couples argue over finances, and 60 percent do not like their partner's spending habits (Sonenshine 2017). Personal finances and, more importantly, spending habits are often a source of contention in many relationships. Let me discuss a unique concept to confront this issue.

While not overly romantic or sexy, Abby and I have monthly "budget or money dates" where we review our financial statements together and how we are progressing with our overall retirement goals. While this budget date allows us to focus on how we are doing concerning our short-term annual goals, it also creates an atmosphere to make decisions on how we can cut back on some areas where we are exceeding our budgeted expense targets. Since Abby and I have always enjoyed having a nice dinner at local restaurants, it comes as no surprise we often exceeded our *dining out* expense line item in our budget, especially since we moved to Philadelphia in the fall of 2021. Thus, the monthly budget allows us to cut back toward the end of the month or ensure we have savings elsewhere. We have found going to early dinner "happy hours" or not ordering wine are excellent ways to save money. The beauty of an overall budget is we often have enough savings in our *groceries* expense budget to offset the dining out overage.

As we edged closer to retirement over the last decade of my working life, Abby and I have concentrated on our net worth statement, which allows us to review our long-term goals and ensures we are on track for achieving our retirement targets. Net worth is the total of our assets (things we *own*) less our total liabilities (things we *owe*). The key assets that lead to a higher net worth include such things as home ownership, retirement savings, and investments (Taylor 2022). Hopefully, as you get older, your assets are growing while your liabilities decline to the state of nirvana with no debt. Through saving efforts and tracking our monthly budget, Abby and I were able to achieve this debt-free nirvana in 2017.

Like many people, Abby dislikes talking about financial stuff. We decided to make our monthly money dates more fun as we usually have a nice dinner with a bottle of wine. This can be at a restaurant or simply at home. You could also do this as a single individual to ensure a periodic financial review. My advice is to make it a fun habit that you will enjoy. You can find the concept of this monthly couple discussion in the book, *What the Happiest Retirees Know,* where the results of a study of over 2,000 older folks revealed: "Happy retirees talked about personal finances with their partners one to two hours per month" (Moss 2022). In my opinion, that is time well spent to achieve combined happiness with our finances.

It is still quite common in this modern day and age for men to handle money or financial issues in their households. In an Ohio State University (OSU) study, men were more likely to be the spouse with the most knowledge of a couple's finances (Grabmeier 2021). According to Sherman Hanna, lead author of the study and OSU professor, men may push to be the primary decision-makers as wealth increases as well as the complexity of their finances. The results have important implications for financial professionals, especially those who work with couples. In an interview with the fellow author as well as the founder and CEO of her financial planning practice, Cassandra Smalley, CFA, CFP, I wanted to hear her thoughts on how we get women to the financial table to be more involved with their finances. She shared the following: "I think the way we approach finances needs to be less about the numbers and more about life planning, security, and peace of mind."

As we learned in my introduction, Frank O'Connell's passing at age forty-eight was challenging for many reasons. Since Frank had always taken care of financial things (as is the case in many households per the OSU study mentioned earlier), it was challenging for his wife, Lisa, to pick up the pieces in light of the crumbling world around her as a grieving widow. As I have personally witnessed when my male family members passed in 2020 to 2021, it is exceedingly difficult for a widow to properly grieve over the loss of her companion while also trying to become a financial decision-maker. Lisa did an amazing job of learning the household finances. I also was able to find an excellent and compassionate financial advisor who was able to assist her with the longer-term issues of investments and retirement.

In speaking with Curt Stauffer, who is president at Seven Summits Capital, LLC in Lancaster, Pennsylvania, about his time with Lisa, he said, "My relationship with Lisa has only grown stronger over time because we have developed a very open and honest relationship." When asked if he could offer any financial advice to others who have recently lost their spouse or significant other, he said, "For the widows, the first two years, on average, are emotionally fragile times for the surviving spouse." He offered great advice as follows: "It is during this time that a financial advisor needs to display understanding and compassion while reassuring them that their financial lives are being watched by someone whom they can trust." A dozen years later, the great news is Curt continues to work with Lisa today, which reflects the long-term bond that can develop with an advisor.

I also interviewed fellow author Cassandra Smalley, who is an award-winning senior wealth manager in St. Petersburg, Florida, and was named "*Forbes* America's Top Women Wealth Advisors 2020–2021." I learned several key concepts about her interactions with couples over the past fifteen years: "I think where it works most beneficial for the couple is when both are engaged in the conversation and can understand the direction that they are both trying to get to." Look for a more insightful discussion on this topic in her book, *The Why of Wealth* (Smalley 2023). Concerning my concept of budget or money dates with your spouse, Cassandra stated, "I think it is a playful way to try to get couples to sit down together."

When I think about Cassandra's profound statement related to understanding the direction of couples, I am curious if there are some areas of our lives that we need to increase our spending and not be constrained by our budgets. In my opinion, any spending on increasing our happiness falls into this category.

Speaking of happiness, my key takeaway from Wendy De La Rosa's TEDx Talk called "10 Steps to Boost Your Financial Health" was when Wendy suggested, "We should increase our spending on happiness." Focus on experiences, spending time with others, and things that save you time (e.g., cleaning your house, mowing your lawn) and increase your happiness. Some of our past expenditures were a bit frivolous. If the spending was reasonable and increased our happiness as a couple, this was money well spent and easy decisions for Abby and me. For example, we love spending money on travel. Our favorite vacations have been going to college basketball games during March Madness in various cities for over twenty-five years. Also, we have shared amazing retirement experiences in Hawaii and Canada as well as numerous trips to the beautiful serene beaches of the Outer Banks (OBX) of North Carolina. We also enjoyed many trips with friends and family, such as fall trips to the beach as well as a Midwest baseball trip with my brother and best friend in 2019, which we will discuss in a later chapter.

In this chapter, we learned about how much net pay we are realizing on our paychecks. In addition, we learned about budgets, budget tools, and the somewhat novel concept of budget dates. While rather basic, I hope the personal finance tips discussed in this chapter help others better understand and discuss their financial matters. If this topic is still confusing, my advice is to speak with a financial advisor, such as Curt or Cassandra. Per the National Association of Personal Financial Advisors (NAPFA) website, you can search for a financial advisor in your area.

During a game of chess, it is imperative to plan your moves in reaction to what you think your opponent's moves will be. When I was playing at my highest level of competition, I would plan at least three to five moves ahead and run through the various permutations of how I would react to different moves by my opponent. The development of this planning skill was helpful to me throughout my life. Keep in mind this chapter's lesson: *With chess, money, and life, failing to plan is planning to fail.*

CHAPTER 8:

HOW DO I PREPARE FOR RETIREMENT?

———

What do you mean our government is not going to take care of us when we get old and retire?

Like many people, I thought if I worked until age sixty-five and relied on the government programs provided by Social Security and Medicare, I would be fine in retirement. As it turns out, it is not that easy.

Per a great TEDx Talk titled "An Honest Look at the Personal Finance Crisis," I learned the three-legged retirement income stool (savings, pensions, and Social Security) has become very wobbly (White 2018). As Elizabeth White further explains, many working families have nothing left after paying their basic bills. She adds, "The median household in the US only has enough savings to replace one month of income, while the recommended level of emergency savings is three to six months." As we learned in the introduction, 32 percent of Americans cannot pull together even $400 to cover an emergency. Unforeseen events like the pandemic job losses, a large medical bill, a new roof, or a flooded basement are good examples of expenses that arise unexpectedly. These examples reflect why we need to do a better job of planning and saving to prevent our own financial crisis, which we can avert by keeping three to six months of expenses in a cash emergency fund.

White went on to say the pension leg is almost nonexistent as only 13 percent of American companies offer them anymore. In its place, we got 401(k) plans and the responsibility for retirement shifted into our laps as well as the risk. With no formal training on this personal finance topic, it turns out we are not particularly good at managing market risk. Half of all Americans have no (zip, zilch, zero) retirement savings at all, while many baby boomers have underfunded their retirement by not investing enough, taking loans against their plans, or withdrawing balances when switching jobs. White went on to say, "Systemic factors have caused an eight trillion retirement income gap."

Lastly, as savings and pensions crumble, many retirees depend on Social Security as their sole retirement plan. According to White, Social Security was never supposed to be our only retirement plan. It was developed in 1935 to replace roughly 40 percent of our preretirement income. Things had changed a lot since 1935 when a twenty-one-year-old male had only a 50 percent chance of living until he was sixty-five. Today, if you are in your late fifties and in reasonably good health, you are probably going to live another twenty to twenty-five years. As a country, America has invested billions of dollars in the diagnosis, treatment, and management of disease to achieve longevity. As White succinctly states, "We haven't invested in the physical infrastructure to ensure that we live not only a long life, but a good one." We will discuss Social Security issues in more detail later in this chapter.

We need help!

I strongly feel the lack of formal personal finance training needs to change. According to the *New York Post*, a bill signed by Governor Ron DeSantis in March 2022 requires all Florida kids to take and pass a basic financial literacy course to graduate from Florida high schools (Algar 2022). The article goes on to say, "An increasing number of states are seeking to incorporate or require financial literacy classes in their schools," which is due to concerns over a lack of basic money management skills among young Americans. This is long overdue.

What else can we do to prepare for retirement? My advice is to consult a financial advisor for more details, as 401(k) plans are employer-based retirement plans funded through payroll deductions before taxes are taken out. The earnings grow tax-free until after the age of fifty-nine and a half to avoid penalties. I learned one of the most powerful personal finance lessons early in my career, compound interest, which is earning interest on top of interest, according to Investopedia (Fernando 2022). From the start of my career at Hershey, I contributed to the company 401(k) plan and took a minimum of 6 percent from my paycheck to maximize the company match, which was 50 percent of my contribution, or an additional 3 percent. My 401(k) balance and wealth grew substantially over the years as a result of this compounding impact.

How much are you contributing to your 401(k) plan, and can you boost your contribution? Although the rules constantly change, you can contribute a maximum of $22,500 in 2023 to your 401(k) plan, or a maximum of $30,000 if you are age fifty or older due to the additional *catch-up* contributions allowed by law. Be mindful that you must pay a 10 percent penalty should you exceed the maximum contribution limit. Check your company's 401(k) plan rules to ensure you are contributing enough to qualify for the company match. Per a 401(k) provider website, the average match is 6 percent in 2022 (Telerski 2022). This website explains how employers are also increasingly recognizing the 401(k) employer match as a powerful incentive to encourage loyalty to the company. It states that in 2022, almost 60 percent of companies have vesting schedules ranging from one to six years before employees can walk away with the full amount of employer-matched funds. This is truly free money. Do not miss out on it.

MAXIMIZING SOCIAL SECURITY

According to Elizabeth White's TEDx Talk, Social Security was a supplement to each American's retirement to help them avoid poverty. White explains the process well as she indicates anyone who has worked at least ten years qualifies for Social Security retirement benefits when they turn age sixty-two. If you want the full benefit you are owed based on your work history, you must wait until your full retirement age (FRA) to sign up. Social Security payments reduce every month you claim benefits from age sixty-two until your FRA. If you sign up at sixty-two, which many Americans do, as shared below, you only receive 70 percent of your full benefit if your FRA is age sixty-seven (or 75 percent if your FRA is age sixty-six). You can search the Social Security website for your full retirement age to determine the timing of your benefits. You can delay benefits past your FRA if you desire larger monthly checks. The Social Security Administration increases your benefit every month that you delay benefits until you reach age seventy. If you wait until your maximum age of seventy to start collecting your benefits, that equates to a yearly increase of 8 percent, which is an attractive guaranteed return.

Per a thought-provoking article on this topic, age sixty-two is the second most popular age to sign up for Social Security at roughly 30 percent. However, the rate has declined steadily from 50 percent in 2005 (Brandon 2022). Surprisingly, age sixty-six is the most popular age at 34 percent, as this is the age when people born between 1943 and 1954 are eligible to claim full Social Security benefits. In the article, Christopher Rhim, who holds the Certified Financial Planner designation, states, "When you take it at your full retirement age (FRA), which for a lot of people retiring today is sixty-six, there are no reductions in retirement benefits." The good news is that people are becoming more educated on this confusing Social Security benefit timing issue, resulting in more people waiting for the higher benefit payouts later.

As my retirement approached in 2021 after a rewarding career, my wife, Abby, and I worked with our financial advisor to determine our streams of income in retirement. As 2022 has taught us, inflation can have a major impact on our retirement needs. Higher prices combined with greater medical expenses in our older years make it critical to ensure our income and investments can support our longer lives.

Since I turned age sixty-two in December 2021, I needed to decide whether I should start collecting Social Security benefits right away. We discussed this with our advisor to lay the groundwork twelve years ago when I was age fifty. Much like the other guy named Brady, who has won many Super Bowl rings, our Tom serves as our quarterback in our financial lives. We met regularly to discuss current issues (e.g., debt paydown plan) as well as longer-term issues (e.g., 401[k] plans, Social Security, and other retirement vehicles) to ensure we were well-prepared for retirement. To increase my benefits overall, I chose to delay my Social Security benefits until at least my full retirement age (FRA) at age sixty-six years and ten months, which will occur in 2026.

Since I am a fairly healthy person with moderate exercise, I feel there is a good chance I will live into my eighties. Assuming I live to age eighty-five and I qualify for the average Social Security benefit of $1,500 per month, my total benefits received will be $325,000 if I start my benefits at FRA versus $290,000 if I started earlier at age sixty-two. As long as I live until age eighty-five, I stand to receive significantly more Social Security benefits than I would by collecting early at age sixty-two.

A retirement blog, "101 Must-Know Retirement Statistics for 2022," states three interesting statistics. The first is 67 percent (or two out of every three) retirees say their most recent employer "failed to help them" adjust to retirement by providing the proper tools and education around the necessary savings. The second is that Social Security is the primary source of income for 79 percent of all retirees and a whopping 93 percent of those over sixty-five. The third shocking statistic is while the average length of retirement is eighteen to twenty years, roughly 60 percent of Americans have no idea of how much they will need for their lengthy retirement period (Rampton 2022).

This shocked me. Am I the only person deeply concerned by the above statistics?

There are several key problems as I see them:

- We thought employers would prepare us for life after working for them (i.e., retirement).
- We assumed our government would take care of our retirement needs through the Social Security and Medicare programs.
- Due to medical improvements and increased focus on exercise, we are living longer in our retirement years.

As a professor, I would give all of us a failing grade of *F* on these first two statements as it is not the sole responsibility of employers or our government to properly prepare us for our retirement stage of life. I staunchly feel it is our responsibility.

In an interesting article, T. Rowe Price (TRP) divides retirees into savers and spenders (Conde 2022). The article breaks them down and discusses the actionable steps you can take to boost your savings. Like Abby and I, savers adjust their spending to maintain and grow their balances. Spenders are retirees who draw down their balances to maintain spending. In the article, TRP's survey reveals 70 percent of retirees identified as savers, while only 30 percent classified themselves as spenders. From the survey, almost 60 percent of retirees said they want to maintain and even grow their assets in retirement. The key to your financial retirement success depends on how well you understand your saving and spending habits.

The TRP survey also indicates longevity, healthcare costs, and inflation as some of the factors that will impact retirement. Thanks to science and medical breakthroughs, we are living longer than ever, but it is costing us more to stay healthy. Inflation in 2022 is at forty-year highs as the COVID-19 pandemic was the primary factor driving excessive inflation in 2022 through demand and supply side distortions. Depending on your savings and spending preferences, you will need to combine different retirement solutions to pay for your financial needs and goals. Here are some common ideas to boost your retirement savings:

1. Maximize the company match for your retirement plan. A Vanguard 2021 study says roughly "one-third (34 percent) of Americans with 401(k) plans are saving below their employee matches" (Geier 2021). In 2023, you can contribute up to $22,500 ($30,000 if you are age fifty and older). This 401(k) match was an important method for building our retirement portfolio and enabling us to retire early.
2. Claim a saver's tax credit. Low- and middle-income taxpayers can qualify for a saver's credit, which offers a maximum credit of $1,000 ($2,000 for joint filers), depending on your adjusted gross income (AGI). Individuals can qualify with an AGI under $36,500 in 2023 ($73,000 for joint filers and $54,750 for heads of household), which updates annually (Conde 2022).

3. Contribute to a Roth IRA to increase retirement savings. If you are over the income thresholds discussed below, increase your savings with a backdoor Roth IRA. If you are a single taxpayer making over $153,000 in 2023, or a joint tax filer making over $228,000, then your income is too high to contribute to a Roth IRA. According to Nerd-wallet.com, a backdoor Roth IRA allows high-income earners to convert pretax contributions into a Roth IRA. They can do this by first contributing to a traditional IRA and then converting that account into a Roth IRA, which is particularly advantageous because retirees do not have to pay taxes when making withdrawals.

4. Boost your retirement savings with a health savings account (HSA). An HSA allows you to put money aside to pay for unexpected medical expenses. Contributions are tax-deductible as long as you spend the money on qualified medical expenses. These expenses include payments to doctors and other medical practitioners, prescriptions and insulin, X-rays and laboratory tests, eyeglasses and contact lenses, and nursing help and hospital care. Any unused funds could continue growing indefinitely, particularly when invested wisely. Abby and I have our HSA invested in low-risk and low-fee stock funds.

Money and finances are not the only aspects of aging and successful retirement. Thus far, I have retired twice, with an early retirement from HE&R in January 2014 after twenty-three years of dedicated service and my second retirement in July 2021 from the University of Illinois after seven years of teaching. As a recent retiree, I firmly believe it is important to focus on other aspects of aging. A pertinent TEDx Talk by Isabel Allende, a novelist who writes stories of passion, discusses three key concepts related to aging, as follows:

1) What do we lose as we age?

"We begin to lose independence, and that scares us." Allende discusses American spiritual teacher Ram Dass, who indicates, "Dependency hurts, but if you accept it, there is less suffering." After an unbelievably bad stroke, his ageless soul watches the changes in the body with tenderness, and he is grateful to the people who help him.

2) What do we gain?

"Freedom, as we don't have to prove anything anymore," Isabel explains. Her body may be falling apart, yet her brain is not, and she has gained spirituality. She states, "While I'm aware that, before, death was in the neighborhood, now, it is next door or in my house." I try my best to love mindfully and be present in the moment.

3) So, how can I stay passionate?

"I have been training for some time as attitude is the key." How do I train? I train by saying yes to whatever comes my way: drama, comedy, tragedy, love, death, and losses. And I train by trying to stay in love (Allende 2014).

Speaking of retirement, the key takeaway for me from Isabel White's TEDx Talk was her parting comment before she left the stage: "On a final note, retirement in Spanish is the word *jubilacion*, which stands for celebration. We have paid our dues, and we have contributed to society. Now it is our time, and it is a great time, so enjoy it."

While many retirees wish they had saved more money for retirement or started earlier, 33 percent of retirees in a recent survey had no financial regrets (Bodnar 2022). The survey indicated 20 percent of retirees are still working because they find part-time work or volunteering to be rewarding. In addition, being in good health and having a partner are also critical factors in retiree satisfaction. The best way to retire without regrets is to follow these steps: save early and consistently, live frugally, pay off debts, and obtain professional advice.

In this discussion on the financial aspects of retirement, we learned about the problems associated with the key parts of retirement (savings, pensions, and Social Security). There are government programs, such as Social Security and Medicare, currently available to assist us when we reach retirement age, subject to changes at the federal level. It is incumbent on each of us to prepare for what should be a celebration time in our lives. With growing concerns about the health of these federally subsidized programs, this chapter presents some helpful ideas on how to boost our retirement savings. Do what seems best for your family and work with a financial advisor.

Preparing for retirement can be hard, but we must also remember to enjoy it. I certainly plan to be happy in our retirement. In the next chapter on the nonfinancial aspects of retirement, I will share more details on how Abby and I are taking on new opportunities in the long-awaited retirement phase of our lives.

Education is the passport to the future, for tomorrow belongs to those who prepare for it today.

—MALCOLM X.

This quote made me think the best chess players are the ones who prepare themselves for the rigors of a long grueling chess match (Malcolm X 2005). As a high school student of this mystifying game, I read every chess book I could get my hands on to learn more about the fascinating game. I truly feel my planning and preparation before a chess tournament were the keys to my success in performing well in many of my matches. Our key lesson is: *Planning is the key to a successful retirement. Enjoy retirement, as it is a six-month holiday, twice a year.*

CHAPTER 9:

AGING AND RETIREMENT

According to a World Health Organization (WHO) report, I am old at age sixty-three.

My research revealed an article from an in-home care group where I learned old age starts at sixty years and above in most developed countries (Sinykin 2021). The article also explains while nobody is immune to the natural process of growing older, adapting to aging is hard for us. The decline in mental and physical health, the death of loved ones, and reduced mobility and socialization opportunities are stressful for most people. Let us delve into this topic and learn what we can do to improve our thoughts on the related concepts of aging and retirement.

Per the above definition, I admit I am old. Thanks to medical science, people are living longer than they ever have before and are active for much longer periods. In Barron's article, AARP CEO Jo Ann Jenkins shared, "Our ability to live longer, healthier, more productive lives is one of humankind's greatest accomplishments. Most sixty-five-year-old folks today will live into their nineties" (Jenkins 2021). While that sounds like great news, the bigger question is, are we prepared for an extended life? The article ponders, "What can we do not only to help people afford their longer lives but to help them thrive as they age?" We need to rethink our attitudes around aging and retirement. As the article states, we are witnessing an exploding consumer market that is bolstering our economy. While we might be old by standard definitions, we baby boomers (those of us born from 1946 through 1964) have lots of discretionary money to spend.

Per Barron's article, the first step is to create a new mindset around aging. While many people are rethinking ways to approach their longer, healthier lives, they fear they may outlive their money. An article from my advisory firm, the Royal Bank of Canada (RBC), states three of the biggest financial threats to your retirement finances are healthcare costs, market volatility, and overspending (RBC 2019). I recommend exercising and using long-term care insurance policies to combat the first threat of rising healthcare costs. Also, we need to develop a diversified portfolio for the second threat, particularly in volatile years like 2022. As discussed in a previous chapter, adhering to a budget is the best way to control your spending. My concepts shared in this section come from our numerous discussions with our RBC financial advisor over the past twenty-five years.

As we learned in our previous chapter, the old model of saving for retirement was the three-legged stool represented by Social Security, individual savings, and employer-provided pensions. If people had these three sources of retirement income, the thought for many retired couples was that they could balance their financial demands and not outlive their money. As Barron's article states, "Although life expectancy continues to increase, individuals and industries have not yet adapted to the need to earn, save, and manage financial resources to support longer lives." As we learned, we need to take ownership of this new way of older life and prepare for our retirement phase as not just saving for retirement but, as the article states, *saving for life*. As we learned from the RBC article, I believe the financial services industry can provide the tools, resources, and solutions people need in this new way of thinking about retirement and beyond.

We have discussed some of the issues surrounding the personal finance crisis and learned some ways to take ownership of our retirement and boost our savings. It is time we turn our attention to other aspects of retirement. While I have discussed how I prepared for our retirement, I also wanted to discover, how do other people prepare for their retirement? Also, I desired to dig a bit deeper by understanding, what are others' reflections on their lives as retirees?

In an interview with Bill Simpson (retired president and CEO of HE&R over five years ago in 2017), he mentioned, "As I neared my retirement date, I started working hard to get some board of director jobs. Being involved with the board at the Woodstock Inn helps me keep active in the hospitality industry." I agree with Bill that staying involved does keep you active in any industry, which is important when you are retired. Bill also added some great advice for approaching the retirement phase of our lives: "One of the things we've talked about is trying to break the next ten years or so into five-year increments. And actually, that was Holly's [his wife's] idea."

In an interview with my wise sister, Shirley, I asked about her career highlight before she retired over twenty-seven years ago in 1995. She said, "My favorite highlight was my teaching career, which I loved as I enjoyed thirty-one years of teaching in a classroom."

Teaching is a common thread in both of our families. This includes three members of our Davis family, with my love of teaching at the college level, Shirley's experiences teaching the elementary school for thirty-one years, and now my intelligent niece, Kylee, currently in her fifth year of teaching history at the high school level in Norfolk, Virginia. On her LinkedIn page, Kylee eloquently states, "Higher education is my end goal to assist others in learning for life and being successful for their dreams" (Davis 2021). I love this phrase as it is very succinct and sums up the focus of teaching quite nicely. In addition, Abby's family has four teachers, including Dustin and Kasey Sheffer, as well as Deb and Libby Warner. While teaching may not be the most lucrative profession, I honestly believe it provided the most rewarding years of my forty-year career.

As we have discussed, retirement is not only about finances. There are other concepts we need to consider about aging. As I mentioned previously, I listened to a TEDx Talk by Isabel Allende, a novelist who writes stories of passion, titled "How to Live Passionately—No Matter Your Age" (Allende 2014). Allende is an expert on aging at seventy-one years old, with her husband being seventy-six. Her parents were well into their late nineties and even her dog, Olivia, at sixteen. I learned from her TEDx Talk, "Society decides when we are old, usually around age sixty-five, when we receive Medicare.

Many of us feel younger than our real age because the spirit never ages. Aging is about attitude and health." This made me think of my aging process, particularly since I had just entered the retirement phase of life.

As previously discussed, I officially retired at the age of sixty-one in the summer of 2021 after a rewarding career of four decades. Abby and I sold our Champaign, Illinois, condo in June 2021 and moved back to the East Coast during the summer to be closer to family and friends. In our monthly money dates, we had discussed our retirement goals as we had planned for this retirement move over a decade ago in 2012 when we bought a beautiful 950-square-foot condo in Center City, Philadelphia, which we rented for the next eight years. After years of rental use by tenants, we began a year-long construction renovation of the Philly condo, which was even more challenging during a pandemic.

I found the initial year of retirement is critical to your overall success and happiness during this phase of life. I dedicated my first full year of retirement in 2022 to fulfilling a bucket list item: writing a book. As I lectured my students often on the virtues of lifelong learning, writing involves discovering new techniques and plenty of challenging work and self-reflection. While I took a five-month book-writing course through Georgetown University at age sixty-two, I am far from the oldest student in my class as my fellow author, Jack, is over eighty years young. I am confident it will fulfill my purpose of paying it forward to my readers, who can benefit from my life lessons and personal finance tips to increase their happiness.

Here are some of my tips for a successful first year of retirement in three key areas:

- Your finances: Adjusting your mindset from building your nest egg to spending it can be challenging. To make your initiation to retiree life easier, create a plan for how you will pay yourself in retirement. Begin by tallying your income sources (e.g., Social Security, 401[k], IRA, pensions) before determining which ones you will tap into first. Next, estimate your cash needs for your first year. Planning this can help ease worries and reduce your risk of overspending. If you need reassurance that your income and cash flow plans are sufficient, meet with a financial advisor. Abby and I meet or speak with our advisory team often, which has been very comforting in our early phase of retirement. Together, you can look at the impact of taxes, evaluate your portfolio diversification, and prepare for the legacy you would like to leave your family and others.

- Your purpose: To start, keep the promises you have made to yourself, your spouse, or others about what your retirement will include. For example, if you have promised distant relatives you will reconnect, then organize a family reunion. Set a date to fulfill your dream vacation or find an instructor who can teach you to play a new sport or start an exercise program. For example, Abby and I completed a ten-day guided trip to four Canadian cities (Toronto, Calgary, Montreal, and Quebec) in the fall of 2022 with eleven interesting and delightful couples from across the US, which was an absolutely wonderful and fun-filled trip.

- Your state of mind: It is normal to feel both excitement and trepidation during your first several months as a new retiree. You are eager for more time to connect with friends and family and do the activities you love. Stepping away from your career can also reduce your stress level and free you from the burden of having competing priorities. However, saying goodbye to your workplace and a regular paycheck may trigger anxiety and sadness. As a nerdy accountant, my biggest challenge was not receiving a monthly paycheck during the fall of 2021 after receiving one for forty years, or 480 months.

For those experiencing mixed feelings, it is helpful to acknowledge them, both to yourself and a partner or trusted friend. Remind yourself why you chose to retire, and remember all you accomplished to reach this point. Then it is time to turn your attention to the things you always wanted to do. This led to regular exercise, spending more time with family and friends, learning a new sport, and writing a book.

I appreciate spending more time with Abby and discovering new offerings in a large city. We love walking to many city sites, such as the great restaurant scene, sporting events on Broad Street, and concerts at the beautiful Kimmel Center, which is only one block from our condo. We also have been able to enjoy the outdoors by bicycling as well as picking up on our new retirement sport of pickleball, which is a racket or paddle sport that combines elements of tennis, badminton, and table tennis. With rising gas prices during 2022, we hope to stay young by walking more often and joining various groups such as city food tours and dinner clubs.

As Isabel Allende discusses in her TEDx Talk, "Aging is about attitude and health." I discussed the healthier aspects of my first year of retirement earlier. As far as attitude, after a year, retirement is going well for me as I accepted a board of director position on the HE&R Employee Support Fund (ESF). This fund provides immediate short-term financial assistance to eligible team members experiencing financial hardship. While I love being part of this ESF committee that has helped numerous employees since its 2003 inception, it also allows me the opportunity to reconnect with some of my favorite coworkers (e.g., Becky, Cami, and Andrea) from my twenty-three years at HE&R.

In her current phase of retirement, Abby assists with local social service agencies in Philadelphia, like Broad Street Ministries, and is now fully involved with a special rowing club on the infamous Schuylkill River. Per their website, Hope Afloat USA is a "rowing program developed specifically for breast cancer survivors helping each other reclaim healthy, joyful lives through the ancient sport of dragon boat racing." This is critical to the cancer recovery process as this program encourages them to be active to boost energy levels that may have dropped during treatment through a healthy and exhilarating sport. I am excited to see Abby participate in this amazing program as it allows her to connect with other women going through similar life experiences. As a bonus, the rowing and coordinated weight-lifting exercise program are excellent for maintaining her fitness levels.

Since I have shared some of my and Abby's retirement experiences, I thought it would be interesting to hear from several other people on how they are dealing with our central themes for this chapter: aging and retirement.

In an interview with my sister, Shirley, I asked her about the most important aspects of her life as she looks forward to turning eighty years young in April 2023. She stays highly active by walking around the historic town of Gettysburg, where she lives, as well as participating in many social and exercise activities at her retirement community. Concerning what she values the most in her wise age, she said, "First of all, family, a very loving family—a family that cared and persuaded us to do the very best we could."

I also interviewed Tim Koller, a retired financial manager with the Certified Financial Planner designation, who was a member of the RBC financial advisory team for Abby and me. He shared his view on what he has enjoyed the most in his retirement over the past three years: "I have never been a person to exercise as I didn't start cycling until age fifty-five. I have grown to like spinning and the camaraderie I built with our spin class." For Tim and I, having the time in retirement to devote to regular exercise is a key to improved aging.

What surprised Tim the most about his retirement, he revealed, was how "we are spending at least what we did prior to retirement and then a little more." While Tim and I both share strong financial backgrounds, we are both spending more in our sixties in retirement than before retirement. Tim said, "This is typical for many couples during the first five to ten years of retirement." A timely article on retiree spending states that in your early retirement years, you may spend as much or even more than you did while you worked, depending on your lifestyle (Curry 2022). The major reason given is higher costs due to travel, inflation, and lifestyle changes, such as dining out more often. Per my budget analysis (as we discussed in an earlier chapter), I would say Abby and I are spending about 5 percent more than anticipated. As we navigate our new city, we are eating out more often, enjoying lots of nearby shows and concerts, and dealing with the highest inflation in over forty years.

And finally, as a financial planner for over thirty years, Tim shared what stood out during his retirement preparation for RBC's variety of clients. He replied, "I think working with people with marginal savings, as a lot of people are not able to save much." Upon my research, I found a CNBC article supporting Tim's comment as the average 401(k) balance of ages sixty-five and older is $255,000, while the median level is only $82,000 (Suknanan 2022). This discrepancy highlights the heavier weighting of the large savers. Using a simple 4 percent rule for withdrawing retirement savings, a $255,000 401(k) balance would generate only about $10,000 per year, which does not allow for a very lavish lifestyle in retirement.

Tim went on to say his greatest financial planning fulfillment came in "finding a better way to give people hope based on government programs such as Social Security and Medicare." While the confusing world of Medicare is outside the scope of this book, please remember some of the key aspects of maximizing our well-earned Social Security benefits from our prior chapter on preparing for retirement. The CNBC article explains the best way to augment your Social Security benefits is to enroll in your employer's 401(k) plan followed by a Roth IRA plan. Per the article, both of these are powerful tools you can use when it comes to saving for retirement since you can contribute after-tax money that gets invested and grows over time.

In delving into the nonfinancial aspects of retirement in this chapter, we learned getting old does not have to be a sad time in our lives. It can be an exhilarating time when we get to do the things we always dreamed of doing. Abby and I have a positive attitude toward aging as retirement has provided us the chance to do things we have dreamed about, such as writing a book, taking a ten-day trip through Canada, or enjoying a new hobby like rowing on a peaceful river on a dragon boat. For others, it may simply mean spending more time with family, volunteering, exercising, taking on civic duties, or just simply sitting at a coffee shop and enjoying a delightful book (like *Checkmate*). I highly suggest by expanding our boundaries as we age and learning new activities, we will only enhance our retirement years and our overall happiness.

Chess was a game I played heavily in my high school days when I had a fair amount of free time. Since I am now retired, I have decided to pick up this fascinating game again. I plan to join a local chess club in 2023, and if I feel adventurous, I may even attend a few chess tournaments in the next year. While I may not be in a position to say it often, the joy of saying *checkmate* at the end of a chess match is an exhilarating aspect of this game. Keep in mind the key lesson: *Age is just a number. New experiences lead to a full life of happiness.*

CHAPTER 10:

OVERCOMING OBSTACLES

One person dies from cardiovascular disease every thirty-six seconds in the United States.

According to the CDC, heart disease causes about 659,000 deaths annually in the US, which is one in every four deaths (CDC n.d.). Heart disease is the leading cause of death for people of most racial and ethnic groups in the United States (Virani 2021). High cholesterol, high blood pressure, and smoking are key risk factors for heart disease. Coming from a family with a history of heart disease, I am currently on medication due to meeting two of the three risk factors (since I am not a smoker). Unlike the famous song by Meat Loaf, this is when two out of three is bad.

We all experience obstacles in our lives, and depending on how we overcome these challenges, they can be great learning experiences for us. As with a game of chess, we deal with many obstacles in life that we cannot plan for. There have been many attacks from my chess opponents I never saw coming. The gauge of success in chess, as in life, is how we overcome these obstacles.

As usual, I was attending my executive committee meeting with our top senior members of the HE&R Company on Tuesday morning, October 18, 2011. In my role as an interim chief financial officer (CFO), I had to attend these meetings, as I was now part of senior management. The meeting started at 8:30, as usual, and I was taking notes when my administrative assistant, Sue McGeehan, God rest her soul, knocked on the door and interrupted our meeting to tell me there was an important phone call requiring my immediate attention. Thinking the worst, I thought something had happened to Abby. The look on Sue's face told me it was something different.

We walked briskly back to my office together, which seemed miles away from my meeting, even though it was only about twenty yards. Once Sue transferred the phone call, I picked up to hear the very distressed sobbing voice of my good friend and coworker's wife as Lisa sobbed, "He's gone, Greg. Frank had a heart attack in the bathroom!" Our dear friend Frank O'Connell was only forty-eight at the time of his death.

In total shock, I tried my best, along with several of Frank's closest coworkers, to comfort Lisa over her sudden loss. It was one of the worst days of my life. Abby and I had just lost a close friend, and our company had lost one of its most important and well-respected managers. Frank had spent thirty-three years with HE&R, rising from a position within the Hersheypark food and beverage department as a teenager to the general manager in charge of the entire Entertainment Group operations.

In an interview with Bill Simpson, COO when Frank passed, I wanted to know what he thought of the aftermath of Frank's passing shortly after the havoc that Tropical Storm Lee had caused our company in the fall of 2011. As you recall from chapter five, this nasty storm provided over twelve inches of rainfall over a three-day period, which caused significant flooding throughout our Hershey properties. After some careful thought, Bill replied, "So, I thought we recovered well from the initial impact of the tropical storm. And then Frank passed, and that just kind of reopened the wound, particularly at the entertainment group."

I spent the rest of that horrible October week assisting Lisa and her family with the funeral arrangements. Frank has two amazing daughters, Aleisha and Ashley, who were incredibly strong in their period of grief. Over the next several months, I dedicated at least one evening per week to Lisa getting her familiarized with running the household, including finances.

I recently listened to a life changing TEDx Talk where Nora McInerny shared her hard-earned wisdom about life and death when she wrote about dealing with grief and loss (McInerny 2019). Nora draws on her personal experience of miscarrying a child and losing both her father and husband to cancer within several weeks in 2014, which sounds similar to my 2020 year. She says, "Usually, when I talk about this period of my life, the reaction I get is essentially, 'I can't—I can't imagine.' But I do think you can, and I think that you should because, someday, it's going to happen to you." Maybe not these losses in a specific order or at this pace, but the research she has seen will stun you. It indicates, "Everyone you love has a 100 percent chance of dying."

Over eleven years later, both Abby and I miss Frank and think about him often. This is particularly true when we hear his favorite artist, Jude Cole, on the radio. After Frank's sudden death, it was a major reset for Abby and me at the end of a difficult 2011. Abby had also experienced some challenging issues in her stressful world of pathology. We had some heavy discussions during the next several months, as Frank's passing served as an eye-opener to our busy lives and caused us to reassess what we wanted out of life. We decided we would wind down our busy careers and try to move into a less intense phase over the next two to four years. As we learned in an earlier chapter, we achieved this goal in 2014 when we moved into a semiretirement phase of our lives.

While some of life's obstacles can hit us in the form of health issues, occasionally our job or career can create major challenges. In our second story, we learn how life's many obstacles can also come from our work or businesses. Most of us say, "It will never happen to my company or me."

According to a recent Association of Certified Fraud Examiners (ACFE) report, US businesses will lose an average of 5 percent of their top-line gross revenues to fraud. The median fraud loss is $100,000 and lasts for roughly a year (Dorris 2022). The ACFE report indicated private companies and small business rank highest in occupational fraud frequency at 42 percent compared to large corporations, governments, and nonprofits. The report also indicates the main contributing factor is the lack of internal controls.

After such a horrendous 2011 in my first full year as interim CFO, I knew 2012 had to be better. It was mid-January 2012 when I received a call from my administrative assistant, Sue, indicating our accounts receivable manager, Derek Sunbury, wanted to come to speak with me in my office as soon as possible. My first thought was that Derek, who was one of our sharp and upcoming finance managers, had probably found another job, and I did not want to lose him.

I had known Derek for over twenty years. He was the son of two of our best friends, Jim and Karen Sunbury, whom I have known for forty years. Being a personable, bright, young hard-working man, it was exciting when Derek came to work for HE&R. Derek had recently earned the prestigious certified fraud examiner (CFE) credential, which is awarded to individuals who have experience in fraud prevention and detection. This was one of many reasons I did not want to lose him at HE&R.

After Sue arranged the meeting with Derek, he drove across town to meet me in my downtown Hershey office. When he entered my office, he was very pale. I knew right away this was not a general chit-chat type of meeting. After some minor pleasantries, Derek told me he ran some reports and discovered an internal fraud where one of our finance employees was stealing money from our company in a credit card scheme. Upon his analysis for the most recent year, 2011, he determined it was at least $30,000 of fraudulent activity.

After hearing this news from Derek, I notified the proper authorities. In one of my worst moments as interim CFO, I walked nervously to my boss's office to notify him. Sitting in Bill Simpson's office, explaining how one of my finance employees was able to steal from the company, was very embarrassing. I felt personally responsible because the fraud had occurred while I was CFO. Fortunately, Bill was a compassionate leader who explained we needed to conduct a full investigation and report to our board of directors the findings and recommendations for fraud prevention in the future.

After weeks of investigation, we determined this employee had been performing this credit card scheme for the past decade and had stolen $333,323 of company funds through electronic transactions. As per the ACFE report mentioned earlier, we determined that this employee theft resulted from a lack of internal controls. The amazing part of the story was this employee was with the company for over twenty-five years, which earned her recognition as a "legacy employee" and a notable achievement in our company. In addition, they named her "employee of the year" in her division twice. If asked, I would have indicated she was one of the least likely employees I would suspect of employee fraud and theft of the seventy full-time employees in our finance department. The research suggests while it may seem counterintuitive, it is often the employees who have been working at a business the longest who are most likely to commit fraud (Dorris 2022).

During a May 2022 interview with Derek, I wanted to understand the key to uncovering this employee theft a decade ago. He said since he was in a new position as accounts receivable manager, "I took it upon myself to build a spreadsheet to see how well our vacation packages were doing. And literally, the sixth day that I started a new review process, a transaction popped up that was a random credit card that had nothing to do with being on that package."

Per an interesting employee theft article, I discovered "37 percent of all embezzlers work in finance or accounting," the "average age of the perpetrator is forty-eight years old," and "56 percent of funds theft is perpetrated by women" (Weisbrot 2022). As it turns out, our accounts receivable clerk, "Mrs. B," was age forty-five at the time of her arrest in April 2012 after a four-month investigation into her fraudulent activity. When speaking with the police, she indicated she was trying to garner additional funds to help offset the cost of medicine for her ailing son.

So far, the sudden loss of a great friend and the shocking discovery of a ten-year fraud by one of our finance employees at HE&R during my time as interim CFO were two of the greatest challenges in my life and career. My final challenge involves the particularly difficult obstacle Abby and I would face years later in 2018.

Abby and I decided to fly back to our families in Pennsylvania for the 2017 Thanksgiving holiday week. These were typically remarkably busy weeks as we spent holiday time visiting with friends and families. On Wednesday morning, Abby was to have her annual mammogram procedure at her doctor's office in York, Pennsylvania, the same hospital group she had worked with as a pathologist. After her test, she received a call from her doctor's office several hours later. They wanted to do a follow-up ultrasound procedure. Then they would meet with her and discuss the results shortly after Thanksgiving.

It is scary to think one in eight US women will develop breast cancer throughout their lifetime. To put this statistic in context, try this two-step exercise: think of eight women you know (e.g., wife, coworkers, friends) and realize out of those eight women, one of your closest female associates will have or has had breast cancer during their lifetime.

Abby, as usual, did not say much about her appointment, yet she seemed out of sorts as we celebrated the holiday by visiting both of our families. At the follow-up meeting, the doctor diagnosed her with Stage 2 breast cancer. When I did the exercise described above, the one female diagnosed with breast cancer was my beautiful and amazing wife, Abby. This was shocking to all of us as Stage 2 means the breast cancer is growing yet still contained in the breast or growth has only extended to the nearby lymph nodes (NBCF 2020). She worked closely with her doctors to set up surgery to remove the cancerous right breast in January 2018.

As you can imagine, this worrisome news over the 2017 holidays made for a taxing next eight weeks in preparation for the surgery. While it was not ideal, we would be 700 miles apart during this critical time. Abby felt most comfortable having this important surgery done by trusted surgeons she knew in the hospital where she had worked for fourteen years. With the support of some amazing cooperative professors in my accountancy department, I was able to take a week off from the critical initial weeks of my University of Illinois classes to be with Abby for her surgery. She would then stay at her sister, Cherie's house, who lived less than ten minutes from York Hospital, during the recuperation phase for the next several months. Special thanks go out to Cherie for her amazing support of her sister during this challenging time.

On January 22, 2018, Abby went through the three-hour single mastectomy, and the surgery went well as expected. Afterward, the surgeon explained they had removed all the cancerous tissue. Subsequent testing determined she would benefit from four cycles of chemotherapy. I had no idea what Abby was in for with this scary procedure.

Chemotherapy is a drug treatment that uses powerful chemicals to kill fast-growing cells, such as cancer, in your body. Though chemotherapy is an effective way to treat many types of cancer, this treatment also carries a risk of side effects, such as nausea, vomiting, diarrhea, hair loss, loss of appetite, and fatigue (Mayo Clinic 2022). If you want an eye-opening experience, join a cancer patient during one of their chemotherapy treatments. I joined Abby in her final treatment. The medical staff wore protective suits while they administered the treatment to the patient intravenously. While it was not painful for Abby, it was a very sobering experience to sit next to her while they injected poison to kill any cancer cells that might remain in her body after her mastectomy.

Like most cancer patients, Abby endured many of the nasty side effects of chemotherapy. She lost her hair and experienced fatigue. Unfortunately, various complications led to Abby having a total of six more surgical procedures over the next eight months of 2018. She also endured a week-long hospital stay in Champaign, Illinois, in the fall due to an infection related to the breast reconstruction process. To say 2018 was a challenging year would be an understatement. The good news is the chemotherapy worked. I am happy to report Abby will be cancer-free for five years in early 2023.

As a spouse of a breast cancer patient, I realized no one teaches you how to endure this terrible disease together. After reading a book that Abby gave me from the local Breast Cancer Foundation, I learned being a caretaker is not easy. However, it is especially important. Not knowing what will happen to your significant other when they are diagnosed with breast cancer is absolutely terrifying and leads to many sleepless nights. I discovered it is normal to feel scared to death every day while fighting this disease. After seeing clumps of hair loss in the shower due to chemotherapy, the best discovery was seeing the real beauty of your wife shine through after Abby had her head shaved. She fiercely fought off this nasty cancer.

As a pathologist who makes breast cancer diagnoses as part of her work, I interviewed Abby on her diagnosis of cancer, and she said, "Although I felt like I remained fairly calm throughout the process, as a pathologist, I think I tended to prepare for the worst-case scenario." Upon asking Abby about how she truly felt during this difficult time in her life, she stated, "However, I was also aware that the vast majority of breast cancer cases are very treatable and most women survive. Nonetheless, it was still a life-altering experience."

In this chapter, we learned of three obstacles I faced during my life, including the final story that relates to how cancer or other health issues can disrupt and impact our lives. Much like a tense game of chess where we face many obstacles (e.g., stronger player, distractions, not feeling well, etc.), overcoming the many obstacles life throws our way teaches us to look for the positive in each one and makes us stronger. For example, while the loss of Frank in 2011 was one of the most challenging obstacles we faced, Abby and I moved into a much happier and slower pace of life when we traded in our busy careers in 2014 to move to Illinois to enjoy semiretirement together. The lesson here is: *While not easy, overcoming obstacles is worth the journey.*

CHAPTER 11:

LEARNING FROM MISTAKES

—

All men make mistakes, but only wise men learn from their mistakes.

—WINSTON CHURCHILL

We all make mistakes or do stupid things at various points in our lives. While I have done some things well in my life, such as marrying Abby, there certainly have been numerous mistakes I have made. I devoted this chapter to sharing them to laugh a little as well as learn from our mistakes.

HOME OWNERSHIP MISTAKES

Regarding the value of do-it-yourself (DIY) projects, I learned with a little sweat equity, home improvements can add real value to your house (Fontinelle 2022). The article indicates upgrading your home does not have to be expensive or complicated, and it does not have to involve costly outside contractors. I thought I would share a DIY story from our early days of home ownership.

Abby and I had just bought and moved into our first house in 1989 in Palmyra, Pennsylvania, which was very exciting for a young couple. We figured as new homeowners, we should do what every first homeowner does: a DIY project. We decided to add some visual space to our condo by adding mirrored tiles on the wall behind our living room gas fireplace. We went to the local hardware store and bought all the necessary materials. Since it was 1989, we did not have "YouTube" videos for assistance. We decided to forge ahead and start the project on a Saturday morning.

It took both of us a while to get a routine down. After a few hours, we were making headway on completing the wall of mirrored tiles until we ran out of caulk. No worries as we drove back to the local Wilhelm's hardware store, where they were immensely helpful. When the store assistant showed us the caulk, he also pulled a caulk gun out of the next bin to see if we needed another one to assist with our mirror wall project. Abby and I looked at each other with disbelief, as we did not know a caulk gun even existed. You guessed it. We had been manually pushing the caulk out of the tube for the past three to four hours.

Sub lesson: Do your homework or speak with an expert before starting a home renovation project.

During the second year of living in our condo in 1990, we discovered the community changed our mailboxes. As usual, I was the first one home on a warm June summer evening as I parked my car near our condo and walked the twenty yards to the mailboxes to get our mail. It surprised me to find I could not access our mail as there was now a protective device covering the block of mailboxes for our neighborhood. I shared this issue with Abby so she could check out the mailbox situation and determine a viable solution. The next night, she arrived home and walked over to the mailboxes, only to discover she was also unable to access our mail due to the protective covering I encountered.

After much discussion, we decided I should call the local United States Postal Service office the next day to make them aware of our recent mail access issues in our neighborhood. I called, and after a short wait I spoke with the local post office representative and explained the issue of this new protective covering, which was preventing us from getting any of our mail. He put me on hold and said he wanted to speak with our neighborhood mail carrier about the new mailboxes. When he returned to my call, I detected a bit of humor in his voice as he stated he "had a solution for our issue." It turns out that when they installed the new mailboxes, they had turned them 180 degrees, so the keyed boxes now faced away from our driveway. In other words, his advice was simply to walk around to the other side of the mailboxes to access our mail.

Sub lesson: Occasionally, we are not able to see the forest for the trees.

Although second home ownership increased during the past several years of the pandemic, they only account for approximately 6 percent of all homes sold in the country. Second homes (i.e., homes sold to buyers who are not going to occupy the home year-round and use it as vacation homes) account for 15 percent of new single-family home sales (Emrath 2021). Many of us dream of owning a second vacation home somewhere on a deserted island. For Abby and I, our island location was in North Carolina.

As we learned earlier in this book, Abby and I loved going to our favorite beach vacation spot, Outer Banks, North Carolina (OBX). After several years of mulling over the purchase of a vacation home, we decided in 2005 to take the plunge. After finding our dream vacation home in a quiet, gated golfing community in Corolla, North Carolina, we moved forward with the financing and other buying costs required to buy this large 4,500-square-foot home.

When reading an article discussing the second home market, I learned buying a second home is a major decision (Wood 2021). This is the case whether you are laying claim to your favorite vacation spot or taking the first step into real estate investment. The costs involved with purchasing and maintaining a second home add up very quickly. I wish I had known more about the true costs of a second home in those days. Continuously paying contractors to fix various issues (e.g., windows, deck replacement, etc.) was a valuable and painful lesson in vacation home ownership.

We were able to pull together the 20 percent down payment and finance the remainder through some creative financing tools. Since it was at the peak of the real estate market for beach properties, our best option was a jumbo mortgage, which is a loan where homeowners must undergo more rigorous credit requirements than those applying for a conventional loan (Crone 2021). During the loose credit policy period of 2005, banks offered multiple option payments for these types of nonconventional mortgage loans. We chose the ability to pay interest only for up to five years, which felt very risky to me as a conservative accountant. Then a more conventional mortgage payment of principal and interest would be due for the remaining twenty-five years. The lax lending standards were one of many reasons that led to the 2008 through 2009 worldwide financial crisis.

While not an ideal financial situation, I knew Abby and I had some sizable bonuses coming from our jobs over the next several years. These bonuses would allow us to pay down the principal on our mortgage, which we did from 2006 through 2008. Then with a much-reduced balance, we could convert to a traditional mortgage at much lower interest rates. In 2017, we sold this house for much less than we had bought it at its peak twelve years earlier, which resulted in a sizable capital loss on our tax returns. While we loved owning a beach house in OBX, this was probably the worst financial decision of our lives. Despite the financial hardship we endured as vacation homeowners, we loved offering our beach home for other family members to use during our twelve years of ownership. For example, my brother, Doug, and his family made at least one to two visits annually to enjoy their favorite vacation, which was going to the beach. Doug drove his family to our beach house in a snowstorm over the holidays one year. He even bought a shovel, which we never used again, as snow is rare in the OBX.

Homeownership lessons: Be aware of the timing when you buy real estate and ensure you fully understand all costs.

CAREER-JOB MISTAKES

I also want to share some lessons I learned from several humorous career mistakes I have made.

I learned tips to prepare for your first interview or any interview in a YouTube video (Juarez 2020). Highlights of the tips included the following:

- Dress the part and be on time.
- Analyze the job and related requirements.
- Do your research on the company.
- Follow-up with a thank-you note. This often forgotten tip was especially important to me. I was a hiring manager for many years and always looked for candidates who took the time to send me a thank-you note or email. In my opinion, if they failed to find the time to write and send me a follow-up note, I was unable to find the time to hire them.

During an interview with Kayvon Asemani, the amazing young man and Milton Hershey student we met earlier in the book, he recalled the advice I gave him during a career day event when he was just a high school sophomore. "You said when people do not take the time to write you a thank-you note on the day of your interview, you do not hire them. With that in mind, I emailed you a thank-you note that night, and you responded, and we have stayed in touch ever since." With these job interview tips in mind, let me share how my first job interview proceeded.

While in my senior year in 1980 at Gettysburg College, the accounting firms called on students for interviews during the fall semester as they preferred to get their hiring out of the way before the busy spring tax season. I received a call from one of the *big eight* accounting firms, defined as the eight largest accounting firms in the world before the 1989 downsizing occurred (Katz 2002). I received an invitation for an interview in Baltimore, Maryland. I was not very comfortable driving or navigating a big city since I grew up in rural Pennsylvania. I should point out to my younger readers this was well before cell phones and navigational systems. In my preparation for the interview, I realized it included a luncheon with several members of the hiring firm. Being both excited and nervous about the whole ordeal, I decided to reach out to my brother-in-law, Wayne, for any luncheon tips, as he held numerous business lunches in his role as a real estate broker. He simply suggested ordering a salad and the *soup du jour*. Thanks to my years of taking French in high school and college, I knew that phrase meant the soup of the day (haha).

Because of Wayne's great advice, I was anxious to show those accounting firm folks just how cultured I was. The morning portion of the interview went okay as I tried to impress them with my high grades in college, yet I fell short of not having many other activities or group functions during my college years. It was a gorgeous crystal-clear warm fall day when we were seated for lunch at a fancy posh restaurant overlooking Baltimore's picturesque Inner Harbor. Upon ordering, I calmly announced I would like a caesar salad as well as the "soup du jour," which the waiter indicated was French onion soup. *Ooh, la la*, I thought. When the soup arrived, I had no idea it had such a thick layer of cheese on top that gave me fits trying to cut through the cheese while attempting and hopelessly failing to enjoy the soup. Let us just say it was an absolute mess to eat as I had cheese all over me after I finished only half of the bowl. The rest of the interview went as poorly as lunch had, and so it was no surprise when I got a rejection letter from them.

For a young man who had grown up in a small rural town, working at a large national firm in a metropolitan city was not the best path for me. Fortunately, I was able to obtain a job at a smaller regional accounting firm in nearby Harrisburg, Pennsylvania. Here is a story from my initial month of working at my first full-time job.

After graduating from Gettysburg College, I worked my first job in June 1981. During the first several weeks of work as a *business professional,* I was excited to drive to my public accounting firm office in Harrisburg, Pennsylvania. On Monday morning, I was sitting in the *bullpen*, which had numerous cubicles together where all the rookie staffers worked when not assigned to an audit assignment in the field. I had just grabbed some tea when the office phone rang around 8:30 a.m. At least ten people were around, and they all ignored the stupid phone. After about twenty-five rings, I could not stand it anymore and walked over to pick up the phone call. Our lead receptionist explained to me that by picking up the phone, I was the *lucky* staff member to get the task of picking up our mailbag from the local post office. *No big deal*, I thought. *How hard can that task be?*

In my new fancy suit, I walked about four blocks to the post office and asked for the mail for my accounting firm, Main Hurdman. It flabbergasted me when they dragged a large bag of mail (which looked like Santa's full bag of toys) out of the back office for me to take back to my firm. It felt unbelievably heavy. I tried to carry it down the street. Nonetheless, I was unable to do so for very long. I resorted to dragging it the rest of the way until I saw the sidewalk had started to burn a hole in the bottom of the bag. When I arrived back at my office, perspiration drenched me as if I had just run the Boston Marathon. Finally, I reached the receptionist's desk. She took one look at me and, with a smirk, said, "Now you know why nobody answers the bullpen phone on a Monday. It is the largest accumulation of mail from the weekend."

Career and job lessons: Live and learn as you cannot beat on-the-job training.

In the world of chess, all players have good games and bad games. Unfortunately, one of my most poorly played games came on the biggest stage in the final round of the National High School Chess Championship in 1977. As I will share in more detail in the next and closing chapter, I made numerous mistakes, or blunders in chess terminology, against my very strong opponent, who was competing for a national championship trophy. While only seventeen at the time, I learned a lot from my mistakes during this memorable, albeit painful, chess match.

I decided to share these humorous stories as it is important to realize we all do stupid things, and in this serious world around us, it is good to laugh at ourselves. The Mayo Clinic's chief medical editor, Dr. Pruthi, indicates, "Laughter is a great form of stress relief as she strongly recommends that all of us put humor on our horizon." The article explains how laughter soothes tensions, improves our immune systems, relieves pain, and increases our satisfaction (Pruthi 2021). As we have heard before, Dr. Pruthi concludes the article by stating, "Laughter is the best medicine."

You can garner tremendous lessons from the silly or stupid things we have done. For example, ordering a soup I had never tried before was not my best interview luncheon decision. More importantly, regarding the lessons we learned in the retirement chapters of this book, buying a beach house at peak prices in 2005 was not a wise financial decision. As we learned from the quote stated at the beginning of this chapter by Winston Churchill, the takeaway lesson for all of us is: *Learn from your mistakes and laugh at yourself.*

CHAPTER 12:

HOW TO ACHIEVE HAPPINESS

———

How happy are you right now in this stressful world we live in?

If you recall from my introduction, according to a recent survey, only 19 percent of American adults say they are very happy (Ingraham 2022). We struggle with being happy. This is severely down from 31 percent of adults who said the same only four years ago in 2018. The worldwide pandemic may partially be a reason for the largest decline since the survey started fifty years ago in 1972. Also, the not-too-happies surged by a nearly identical amount, from 13 percent to 24 percent. These latest statistics led me to a major theme in this book: How happy are you, and what can we do to increase our happiness?

I can say with 100 percent confidence that I have lived a happy life.

In my 1977 high school yearbook, my ambition was "to be happy and successful." Sure, lots of things have gone wrong in my life, which you have read about, and I could have done a few things much differently. As I reflect on my life and career at age sixty-three, it turns out I am pretty damn happy. In this chapter, I will share some of my favorite stories on this important topic of happiness. Earlier in my book, we met futurist, Dominic (Dom) Price, who seeks to build a happier, more effective, and more balanced future while he currently works at a software company.

I love Dom's quote in his TEDx Talk: "What is really important to all of us on our deathbed is the love of friends and family, the legacy you're leaving behind, knowing that you have done things that made you and others happy" (Price 2021). Yet few of us can say this is how we are living our lives. As Dom indicates, "You need to take a personal moral inventory, where we review our scores in four areas, as follows, that is the secret to our happiness."

- Productivity and Profit—job, salary, house (material stuff).
- People—your personal, mental, and physical health.
- Planet—impact on the environment (air and car travel, etc.)—carbon footprint.
- Purpose—the impact you want to have and the legacy you want to leave behind.

Dom's TEDx Talk made me realize this book is my purpose, and it has taken me over six decades to get to the point of having the time and desire to share my tips and techniques to make an impact and leave my legacy behind for others to follow. Dom's discussion also made me reflect on some of the happiest memories in my life involving other people, which revolved around two of my passions: chess and baseball. While my greatest passion is spending time with Abby, one of my best memories and lessons was from my days at Bermudian Springs High School.

As discussed previously, my brother Doug set an exceedingly high standard for me in my formative years. While he was valedictorian in his high school class, I finished a step behind as a salutatorian. Like my brother, I was very popular in high school, as I liked being part of a small graduating class of 105 students and knew every one of my fellow students. In my sophomore year of high school, I joined the chess club when the United States was caught up in the Bobby Fischer craze. He was the first American to become the world chess champion from 1972 to 1975. I read every chess book I could get my hands on and studied them in my free time. I found myself mesmerized by this challenging, thought-provoking game. My love for chess started in 1974 when I learned the game playing with my good friends, Kai and Jeff, in high school.

So how complex is the game of chess? There are over 318 billion different possible positions after just four moves from each player. The number of distinct forty-move games in chess is far greater than the number of electrons in the observable universe (Markushan 2011). This is why I find the game of chess so exhilarating. Even in my sixties, I play several games weekly online as I try to keep my mind sharp. Psychologists often cite chess as an effective way to improve memory function. Allowing the mind to solve complex problems and work through ideas, it is no wonder chess is a recommendation in the fight against the dreaded Alzheimer's disease (Joy 2020).

The highlight of my school years was in my senior year in high school when our five-member chess team went to Cleveland, Ohio, for the National High School Chess Championship. This tournament consisted of 530 chess players from across the country playing eight exhausting rounds over a long weekend. There were two sections of players and teams: an open section, which consisted of larger urban schools, and a novice section, which consisted of smaller schools with an attendance of less than 500 in their grades of nine through twelve. Thanks to our small school size, they placed us in the novice section.

Our team had a blast in Cleveland since none of us had ever been there previously. Our amazing mentor, Coach Vince Kowalski (our "Coach K" before the immortal Duke coach appeared on the men's college basketball scene), was making sure we had fun seeing the sites in this big city for us rural kids from the farmlands of Pennsylvania. After seven rounds, our team was in first place. We enjoyed a one-and-a-half point lead, which was considered a large lead when only four team points were available each round. The rules were a win earned one point while a draw, or tie, earned half a point.

Amazingly, I was playing the best chess of my life. I had gone undefeated after the first seven rounds. Thus, my record was a perfect 7–0 going into the eighth and final round. As was customary in these types of national chess tournaments, the best players would move closer to the front of the large hall after each round. They matched me up against an extraordinarily strong player, Prashant Balwally from Ohio, in the eighth and final round, who was undefeated with six wins and one draw. Since we were both undefeated and the top two players, they seated us in a glass-enclosed room to play our final championship game. With cameras showing our every move while it was telecast so others could watch us play outside of the large hall, it was extremely unnerving. To add to the pressure, tournament officials told me if I won my last match, I would become the first player to post a perfect score in national high school chess history.

Forty-five years later, in my May 2022 interview with Coach K about what advice he gave me before my final match, he said, "All I can say is that I had so much respect for you and your common sense that I just felt very comfortable saying that, you know, do the best you can and do what you feel is best."

Despite Coach K's helpful advice, I was extremely nervous. I felt the pressure of trying to lead my team to a National Championship. Even though a draw would have garnered me the individual championship trophy, I focused on playing for a win for my team and the overall team championship. Coach K reminded me in our interview that our team was not doing particularly well in the early part of the final round, as several of my teammates were in losing scenarios with their opponents. My style of playing chess was typically a very defensive one where I won many games after my opponent would make a blunder, which is an error in chess terms, upon which I would capitalize on it in a winning manner. For some reason, I went on an overly aggressive attack in this championship game. Unfortunately, Prashant being the excellent player that he was, took full advantage of my reckless attack as he defended his position and defeated me in a three-hour match.

You may learn much more from a game you lose than from a game you win.

—RAÚL CAPABLANCA (MACKAY 2017).

At age seventeen, it was a difficult and humiliating defeat for me. Coach K and my team comforted me and made me feel better. While I finished second in the individual championship to Prashant, the best part was my other team members pulled together and won or drew their final matches. The team rallied support behind each other and won the team championship. Upon our return to school, we were celebrities for a week. Local newspapers interviewed us and hailed us as heroes in our small school. At this early stage in my life, I realized teamwork could lead to amazing accomplishments.

In my interview with Coach K about the impact of winning this national title, Vince indicated, "It made me incredibly proud of our school and the kids as it was just something that a young group of kids from a rural school can take on some of the most prestigious schools at that time (e.g., charter schools, private schools) in the country and compete."

In addition to my chess hobby, I particularly love the American pastime of baseball. For me, a good day is going to a baseball game with my wife or friends, having a hot dog and a cold beverage on a summer day or evening.

As I mentioned earlier, my brother Doug and I loved going to baseball games together. Our baseball trips usually included my best friend, Bryan. He became remarkably close to Doug over the years as they shared similar experiences in raising two well-grounded daughters, which is challenging in this world. Since I lived in Pennsylvania most of my life, we would often go to minor league baseball games in nearby York, Pennsylvania, or we would travel a bit further to see one of our favorite major league teams, the Baltimore Orioles. This two-hour trip usually involved a dinner somewhere before the game so we could also catch up on our lives over a nutritional dinner of wings, beer, and soda. The *coup de grâce* trip came during the summer of 2019 when I talked them into joining me for a Midwest baseball extravaganza trip of a lifetime while I was teaching and living in Champaign, Illinois. During this whirlwind baseball tour, we saw three games over just four days.

Bryan and Doug flew into the Indianapolis Indiana Airport on Tuesday, July 30, 2019, where I picked them up. We stayed at the beautiful downtown Marriott in a suite that allowed us to enjoy the concierge lounge on the top floor, which entitled us to free appetizers and drinks. To start the trip off in good fashion, I treated them to a wonderful steak dinner at our favorite downtown restaurant, St. Elmo Steak House. Our first evening game featured the Indianapolis Indians, a minor league affiliate of the Pittsburgh Pirates, in their beautiful stadium, which was located directly across the street from our Marriott hotel. We were living like kings for a week as the "baseball gods" were sharing their happiness with us.

Day two consisted of getting up early and driving three and a half hours to St. Louis, Missouri, for our second game, which featured a Midwest baseball rivalry between the St. Louis Cardinals versus my beloved Chicago Cubs. Once again, I booked a suite in a hotel directly across the street from beautiful Busch Stadium, and they treated us to a wonderful buffet in their concierge lounge featuring wings and beer. The evening was perfect for a baseball game as the Cubs won a close 2–1 victory.

Day three was our travel day as we drove three hours back to our condo in Champaign, Illinois, and spent the day navigating the cool college town, which included the beautiful University of Illinois campus. Catching up with our lives as we enjoyed dinner and drinks in the soothing warm August weather was a nice break from watching baseball.

Being an ardent baseball fan, I love reading about the history of baseball. Wrigley Field, built in 1914, is the second oldest stadium only behind Fenway Park in Boston (Ralpheal 2020). Wrigley Field is the only major league ballpark to feature ivy on its outfield walls. The article also states before 1988, Wrigley Field had no lights, which meant the Chicago Cubs had to play all their home games during the day. Even today, with lights, the Cubs maintain the tradition of day games with more matinees than any other team in baseball. Thus, I felt it was fitting we ended our baseball trip by attending a day game in Chicago's iconic Wrigley Field.

Day four involved catching an Amtrak train from Champaign to Chicago in the morning. We stayed at the beautiful Hilton Conrad hotel in downtown Chicago as we would need to take the subway (the "L") out to the stadium. We were staying only two blocks away from Jake Melnick's Corner

Tap restaurant, which is famous for—you guessed it—wings. We ate lunch and then headed out to iconic Wrigley Field for a great match-up of divisional rivals, the Chicago Cubs versus the Milwaukee Brewers. Again, we experienced perfect summer weather and saw another Cubs 6–2 win.

In an interview with Bryan on his thoughts about this memorable baseball trip, he eloquently stated, "It would have been easy to let the day-to-day rigors of work and family prevent me from making this trip, but something told me to make the effort, and I'm very glad I did." Bryan went on to add, "Taking time to tour the Midwest and attend baseball games along the way with two of my best friends turned out to be a valued lifelong memory."

After watching three baseball games over just four days, the trip came to an end when Doug and Bryan flew out of Chicago O'Hare airport to Pennsylvania. I took the Amtrak train back to Champaign, Illinois. It was truly the baseball experience of a lifetime. We talked about our busy lives, ate well, and added a few pounds. We stayed at some of the nicest hotels in the Midwest and watched some great baseball games in iconic stadiums. While we learned the valuable lesson of "never regret spending time with your family" in an earlier chapter, this 2019 baseball trip with my brother and best friend was one I will always cherish, particularly knowing Doug passed away just over a year later in a tragic vehicle accident.

After doing some research, I found a great article on ways we can increase our happiness (Brooks 2022). An international team of scholars came up with their top simple ways to be happier:

- Invest in family and friends (e.g., 2019 baseball trip or refer back to my first chapter on family).
- Join a club or team (e.g., Abby becoming a member of a breast cancer survivor dragon boat team has been very uplifting for her throughout 2022).
- Get physical exercise (going to the gym, walking, and bicycling work for me).
- Act nicely and smile, which is a daily activity for me.
- Be mentally and physically active (take a walk, play a game of chess, or read a book, such as *Checkmate*).

In summary, this chapter started with depressing statistics about how unhappy we are in our lives. Since it is a central theme throughout this book, happiness is something we need to seek out. Many things make me happy, such as spending time with Abby and our families, going to baseball games or concerts, playing games such as chess and pickleball, and enjoying an excellent dinner at a great restaurant. Your task is to find something you enjoy and make time for it in your busy schedule to increase your happiness. My final chapter lesson is: *Teamwork leads to better results.* My bonus lesson is: *Find something you love to increase your happiness!*

REFLECTIONS

———

Checkmate: Happiness achieved!

Chess players know only too well the excitement we experience when they can announce "checkmate" at the successful conclusion of a long chess match. Similarly, we have come to the end of our journey together by sharing numerous stories, tips, and lessons designed to help you increase your happiness. My primary desire for writing this book was that every reader could benefit from implementing at least one or more of my ideas.

Thanks for completing this journey with me, as we have covered many topics and should review our takeaways. As I reflect on my book journey over the past year, I see this was one of my life's most challenging yet rewarding experiences. Let us recap some of the highlights of the book. We started our journey with me sobbing alone in my hotel room 3,000 miles away from home and realizing I may have made a mistake in leaving a job that involved a wonderful mission in Hershey to pursue a career change in academia at age fifty-three.

The depressing statistic, shared in my introduction, that less than one in five Americans say they are "very happy" is why I decided now is the perfect time to write this book. In this incredibly stressful world, it is challenging for us to overcome obstacles (e.g., job stress, money concerns, and family issues) through perseverance to seek happiness. My perspective is unique as I have been successful in both the corporate world at Hershey as well as in academia as a college professor at the University of Illinois. My ultimate goal was to share my stories, enhanced by research and numerous interviews, which were designed to help you increase your happiness. Let us summarize what we have discovered in each of my chapters before tackling my "challenge" to each of you.

We discussed my rural upbringing in a loving family in the first chapter as well as how tragedy has impacted my family.

Lesson #1: *Never regret spending time with your family and remember those who leave us.*

Next, we tackled a challenging topic for many of us: relationships. After years of unsuccessful dating, I married "the one for me" in May 1990. While marriage is analogous to a Hersheypark roller coaster with lots of ups and downs, I have been very blessed to have Abby in my life.

Lesson #2: *Take your time to find a good life partner to enhance your happiness.*

In the third chapter, we discovered how two men (Milton Hershey and Kayvon Asemani) overcame adversity and used perseverance to make a lasting impact on others' lives. I also shared how the mission to support the amazing Milton Hershey School led to my lengthy career at Hershey.

Lesson #3: *Work for a company that means more than just a paycheck.*

Next, we unearthed how I bounced around various job positions for the first decade of my career until I found the right fit at Hershey Entertainment & Resorts.

Lesson #4: *Find a job that has special meaning, even if it takes a long time!*

In chapter five, we learned how I achieved my career goal of serving as CFO with its challenges in 2011. We also learned in this chapter how I failed miserably at my first attempt at online college teaching. Only two years later, through perseverance, hard work, and lots of support from other professionals, I developed and delivered two online courses that have had great success as well as worldwide impact.

Lesson #5: *Stepping outside your comfort zone to achieve career goals is hard yet rewarding, and it is okay to say no.*

As a follow-up to my introduction, we discussed in this chapter how changing my career path from finance executive to being a college professor was more challenging than anticipated. It led to seven of the most rewarding and happiest years of my career.

Lesson #6: *A career change is hard work, yet finding a job you love is worth the effort!*

In the next chapter, we delved into the confusing world of personal finance, where I shared some basic tips on paychecks, taxes, budgets, retirement savings, and concepts that have aided Abby and me on our path to retirement.

Lesson #7: *With chess, money, and life, failing to plan is planning to fail.*

In chapter eight, we tackled an especially important and confusing topic for all of us: retirement preparation. We learned the three-legged retirement income stool is wobbly as the responsibility for retirement has shifted to us. We shared tips to maximize company-sponsored 401(k) plans, key decisions on when to take Social Security, as well as ways to boost your retirement savings.

Lesson #8: *Planning is the key to a successful retirement. Enjoy retirement as it is a six-month holiday, twice a year.*

In the next chapter, we turn our attention to the nonfinancial aspects of retirement with a discussion on aging and how we should look at getting older positively. Based on my recent experience, I shared my tips for a successful first year of retirement.

Lesson #9: *Age is just a number. New experiences lead to a full life of happiness.*

Like my readers, we then discovered in the next chapter how I had to overcome many obstacles in my life. This included dealing with the grief of the sudden unexpected loss of a great friend, which turned out to be a life-changing event for Abby and me. The second story relates how fraud has permeated our society, and we ended this emotional chapter with the story of supporting my beautiful wife, Abby, as she battled breast cancer in 2018.

Lesson #10: *While not easy, overcoming obstacles is worth the journey.*

After such an emotional prior chapter, we took a humorous turn in the eleventh chapter when we discussed how I learned from the various stupid things or mistakes I have done or made in my life. Who knew a caulk gun was such a time saver and *soup du jour* can be quite messy?

Lesson #11: *Learn from your mistakes and laugh at yourself.*

Finally, we ended the book with a discussion of my book's central theme of happiness and its importance in our lives. I shared two of my favorite memories and lessons in my life, from our high school chess championship in 1977 and our Midwest baseball trip in 2019.

Lesson #12: *Teamwork leads to better results.*

Bonus Lesson: *Find something you love to increase your happiness!*

In summation, I truly hope you have enjoyed reading this book as much as I have loved the challenge and experience of writing it over the past year. As I stated in the introduction, "Perseverance is the key to overcoming obstacles in our lives to achieve our dreams." For example, writing a book was challenging, yet the desire to share some of my experiences with the sincere hope of having my readers increase their happiness has been my driving force. It seems fitting I would end this book with a quote by Milton Hershey, as he said, "One is only happy in proportion as he makes others feel happy" (Kraft 2014).

As my Illinois students know well, my special gift is that I now have a "homework assignment" for each of you, as follows: Apply at least two of the lessons in my book to your life. Whether it is making a long overdue career change to a job you love, spending more time (not just holidays) with family, learning from your mistakes, doing something that makes you happy, or saving money by sticking to a budget and investing the extra money into your long-awaited retirement—start today. When you have completed my assignment, I would respectfully request you share your experiences from my book with me at my personal email: gdavis243@comcast.net.

As I have with playing chess as well as authoring this book, enjoy the game of life and seek happiness in your heart!

ACKNOWLEDGMENTS

If you read through this book to the end and have reached this page, you need to be acknowledged, and you should yell out, *Checkmate*!

I ran into roadblocks at several points during the journey of writing this book. My biggest challenge was sitting still long enough to get all my thoughts out of my head and onto a laptop in some semblance of order. Doing so meant being absent and sacrificing time with my loved ones, especially Abby. To members of the Davis and Warner family who encouraged my writing process, were the first folks to pre-order my book, and supported me every step of the way, I am forever grateful.

Abby, the queen of my chessboard, you have earned a round of applause as you had a front-row seat to all the moodiness, frustration, procrastination, and early mornings. Without your patience, love, and willingness to survive through the past fourteen months, there would be no book. You have always supported me, even when I made it difficult for you.

Bill, you have been my mentor, a consistent voice of reason, a trusted advisor, and an inspiration. You remind me to find joy in everything and to never settle for less than exceptional.

Cassandra, John, Sarah, and Marcia, I am very thankful for you reading my entire book and providing comments and feedback. Thanks for making me and my book better. I could not have done this without your valuable input. I also want to express my gratitude to Jo Ann "Coach" Lightman for reviewing the sentimental portions of the book.

I would like to thank Professor Eric Koester from Georgetown University for allowing me to become part of his amazing Book Creators program, which is a unique book-writing program combining instruction, individual coaching, and community. To the team at New Degree Press, thank you for providing a platform to bring my book to life, as Ty Mall, Ken Cain, Brian Bies, and Sherman Morrison deserve special thanks. Thanks for your calming presence, your sharp eye, your steady commitment to keeping me accountable to myself, and your constant reassurance.

Next, I wanted to thank my students, professors, and coworkers at the University of Illinois at Urbana-Champaign for supporting my book as well as providing seven rewarding years of experiences during my academic career. Also, I need to give special thanks to my fellow employees at Hershey Entertainment & Resorts Company for being supportive of my book-writing efforts as well as providing love, support, and friendship to both Abby and me.

While writing this book during the year 2022, I was saddened to hear the unfortunate news that the Hershey organization lost two members: Scott Newkam, retired president and CEO, as well as Sue McGeehan, retired executive administrative assistant. Both of these dedicated coworkers were influential to the success of my Hershey career and will be greatly missed.

A community of over 120 people believed in me so fervently that they made this book possible. They preordered their copies during my presale campaign and helped promote the book before it even went to print. Thanks in particular to my fellow University of Illinois professor, Angel Chatterton, and my lifelong financial adviser, Tom Zielinski, for providing the top tier of financial support for my book funding campaign. I cannot determine what the heck you are planning to do with ten copies of my book, but I hope they bring joy to whoever receives them.

Thanks to all of you, many of whom read excerpts from my early manuscript and gave input on the book title and cover. You are amazing, and as promised, I mention you in my book (listed in alphabetical order by last name):

Henry Ahn

Michael Aiello

Ernie Alviani

Zeynep Baris

Chris Barrett

Christopher Billing

Jennie Byrne

Mary Ann Casner

Cindy Chan

Angel Chatterton

Mariza Cooper

Kari Cooperider

Abby Davis

Kylee Davis

Lynn Davis

Jon Davis

Laura Davis
Lisa DeAngelis
Philip Dearing
Nate Douty
Jorden Drought
Andrea Dusthimer
Sarah El Zayyat
Rich Excell
Ralph Fetrow
Cherie and Paul Flaherty
Christie Gabbay
Kamila Glowa
Alexa Gorowska
Patrick Grant
Marcela Guzman
Amanda Haffly
Brian Hamm
Betsy Hamm
Lindsey Hauch
Heather Heffernan
Eric Hegemann
Marshal Herrmann
Crystal Hoffman
Abby Hohf
Renee Holloman
Kong Hu
Cami James
Liam Kahanic
Kishyori Kamaludin
Lisa Kentner
Jeff King
Grace Klevorn

Eric Koester
Alex Kogen
Timothy Koller
Vince Kowalski
Abraham Lacayo-Morales
Tjibbe Lambers
Dave Lavery
Kiara Lenhardt
Howard Lightman
Sarah Lightman
Jay Livesay
Wayllon Lu
Kristi and Ian Lynch
Marc Malmquist
Sharon Manton
Emily Martin
Kurtis Mayz
Wendy McClintock
Damon McFall
Brian McGinnis
Brian McKeown
Scott and Kim Mendoza
Jim Miles
Jared Minor
Linda Mock
Cristian Munarriz
Dianne Nixon
Shirley Ogburn
Todd Pagliarulo
Mark Panassow
Manish Pathak
Michael Peterson

Lauren Pilla
John Powell
Becky Price
Naveen Rapaka
Bev Reindollar
Matt and Candie Rodgers
Shah Salomov
Kim Schaller
Kiara Schuh
William Sheaffer
Kasey and Dustin Sheffer
Lani Sherman
Kevin Shih
Dawn Shook
Bill & Holly Simpson
Cheryl Simpson
Joe Skrabacz
Cassandra Smalley
Barry Smith
Zack Smith
Bryan Stambaugh
Curt Stauffer
Cindy Steward
Paul Striepling
Kevin Stumpf
Jim and Karen Sunbury
Derek Sunbury
Ron Suski
Rodney Thomas
John Thompson III
Rob van den Blink
Varsha Venkatraman

Emma Wang
Zach Wang
Libby Warner
Deb Warner
Johnny Wheeler
Douglas Winter
Bill Young
Thomas Zielinski
Miriam Zylberglait

APPENDIX

———

INTRODUCTION:

Adamczyk, Alicia. 2022. "A record 68% of American households said their savings could cover a $400 emergency in 2021." *Fortune.* May 23, 2022. https://fortune.com/2022/05/23/record-number-american-households-400-dollar-emergency-savings.

Deer, Paul. 2022. "The Average 401k Balance By Age." *Daily Capital* (blog), *Personal Capital.* September 7, 2022. https://www.personalcapital.com/blog/retirement-planning/average-401k-balance-age.

Ingraham, David. 2022. "New data shows Americans more miserable than we've been in half a century." *The Why Axis.* January 28, 2022. https://thewhyaxis.substack.com/p/new-data-shows-americans-more-miserable.

Jurs, Mike. 2015. "American Employees: Are You Leaving Money On The Table?" *WordPress* (blog), *Financial Engines.* May 12, 2015. https://financialengines.wordpress.com/2015/05/12/employer_match_results.

Leonhardt, Megan. 2021. "Job-hopping heats up: 65% of US workers are looking for a new job." *Fortune.* August 20, 2021. https://fortune.com/2021/08/20/us-workers-looking-for-jobs.

CHAPTER 1:

CDC (Center for Disease Control). 2022. "Daily Update for the United States." Accessed May 2022. https://covid.cdc.gov/covid-data-tracker/#datatracker-home.

Davis, Greg. 1969. *An Autobiography of My Life.* Unpublished.

MHA (Mental Health America). n.d. "Bereavement and Grief." Accessed April 2022. https://www.mhanational.org/bereavement-and-grief.

Moeller, Philip. 2012. "Families Are Changing, But Still Key to Happiness." *U.S. News & World Report.* April 2, 2012. https://money.usnews.com/money/personal-finance/articles/2012/04/02/families-are-changing-but-still-key-to-happiness.

Price, Dominic. 2021. "What's your happiness score?" Filmed May 2021 in Sydney. TED video, 14:46. https://www.youtube.com/watch?v=ejQsLQvfnX4.

Ware, Bonnie. 2019. *The Top Five Regrets of Dying.* Australia, US & UK: Hay House.

CHAPTER 2:

Buchholz, Katherina. 2020. "How Couples Met." *Statista.* February 13, 2020. https://www.statista.com/chart/20822/way-of-meeting-partner-heterosexual-us-couples.

Diamond, Maya. 2019. "The Surprising Key to Building a Healthy Relationship that Lasts." Filmed February 2019 in Oakland, CA. TED video, 8:32. https://www.ted.com/talks/maya_diamond_the_surprising key to_building_a_healthy_relationship_that_lasts.

Lake, Rebecca. 2022. "What is the Average Age of Marriage in the US" *Brides.* April 22, 2022. https://www.brides.com/what-is-the-average-age-of-marriage-in-the-u-s-4685727.

Sullivan, Colleen. 2021. "Marriage Secrets From Couples That Have Been Together 25 Years or More." *Brides.* August 11, 2021.

https://www.brides.com/marriage-secrets-from-married-couples-5184605.

CHAPTER 3:

Asemani, Kayvon. 2018. "Want to win? Stop trying to beat other people." Filmed May 31, 2018, in Philadelphia, PA. TED video, 12:44. https://www.youtube.com/watch?v=CAdywuyVSBk.

Juetton, Mary. 2020. "The Importance of Perseverance." *Forbes.* January 23, 2020. https://www.forbes.com/sites/maryjuetten/2020/01/23/the-importance-of-perseverance.

Kelly, Debra. 2021. "The Untold Truth of Hershey." *Mashed.* October 18, 2021. https://www.mashed.com/112889/untold-truth-hershey.

Kolmer, Chris. 2022. "Average Number of Jobs in a Lifetime:2022." *Zippia.* April 5, 2022. https://www.zippia.com/advice/average-number-jobs-in-lifetime.

Rierdon, Kevin. 2021. "Tragedy made this Penn Wharton grad an orphan, but hard work and talent make him a rising star." *Philadelphia Inquirer.* February 3, 2021. https://www.inquirer.com/life/kayvon-asemani-wharton-milton-hershey-facebook-20210203.html.

Robbins, Tony. n.d. "Don't Give Up on Your Dreams." Tony Robbins. Accessed September 2022. https://www.tonyrobbins.com/mind-meaning/giving-up-on-dreams.

CHAPTER 4:

Caporal, Jack. 2022. "Here's Why 20% of Americans Have Changed Jobs Since the Pandemic Began." *Motley Fool.* January 4, 2022. https://www.fool.com/research/20-percent-americans-changed-careers.

DOL (Department of Labor). n.d. "Career Change Statistics." Accessed March 2022. https://careers-advice-online.com/career-change-statistics.

Doyle, Allison. 2020. "How Often Do People Change Jobs During Their Career." *The Balance.* June 15, 2020. https://www.thebalancecareers.com/how-often-do-people-change-jobs-2060467.

CNN. 2020. *Transcript: Michelle Obama's DNC Speech.* August 18, 2020. https://www.cnn.com/2020/08/17/politics/michelle-obama-speech-transcript/index.html

Kolmer, Chris. 2022. "Average Number of Jobs in a Lifetime:2022." *Zippia.* April 5, 2022. https://www.zippia.com/advice/average-number-jobs-in-lifetime.

Odogwu, Chris. 2022. "How to Say "No" at Work Politely." *Make Use Of.* May 5, 2022. https://www.makeuseof.com/how-to-say-no-at-work.

Shannon, Joel. 2017. "Why wait? How to avoid the long lines at Hersheypark." *York Daily Record.* August 3, 2017. https://www.ydr.com/story/news/2017/08/03/why-wait-how-avoid-lines-hersheypark/535923001.

Vaughn, Kassandra. 2018. "You will spend 90,000 hours of your lifetime at work. Are you happy?" *Medium.* May 5, 2018. https://kassandravaughn.medium.com/you-will-spend-90-000-hours-of-your-lifetime-at-work-are-you-happy-5a2b5b0120ff.

CHAPTER 5:

Castrillon, Caroline. 2020. "This is How Highly Successful People Achieve Their Goals." *Forbes.* March 15, 2020. https://www.forbes.com/sites/carolinecastrillon/2020/03/15/this-is-how-highly-successful-people-achieve-career-goals.

Clarey, Christopher. 2019. "Bianca Andreescu wins the US Open, Defeating Serena Williams." *New York Times.* September 7,

2019. https://www.nytimes.com/2019/09/07/sports/tennis/us-open-serena-williams-bianca-andreescu.html.

Edmondson, Amy. 2020. "How to lead in a crisis." Filmed October 26, 2020, in New York, NY. TED video, 4:34. https://www.ted.com/talks/amy_c_edmondson_how_to_lead_in_a_crisis.

Grumm, Richard H. 2011. "Heavy rainfall associated frontal interactions with Tropical Storm Lee." *National Weather Service.* September 2011. https://www.weather.gov/ctp/TSLeeFlooding.

Jordan, Katy. 2015. "Massive Open Online Course Completion Rates Revisited: Assessment, Length and Attrition." *Eric.* International Review of Research in Open and Distributed Learning Volume 16, Number 3. June 2015. https://files.eric.ed.gov/fulltext/EJ1067937.pdf.

Martins, Julia. 2022. "How to write SMART goals (and why they matter)." *Asana.* July 9, 2022. https://asana.com/resources/smart-goals.

CHAPTER 6:

Berger, Adam. 2019. "Why a Career Change at 30 and Beyond Is So Hard." *Medium.* April 21, 2019. https://medium.com/swlh/why-a-career-change-at-30-and-beyond-is-so-hard-120e7c72d697.

Dickler, Jessica. 2021. "Amid the 'Great Resignation,' Just 7% of Americans say they have their dream job, survey finds." *CNBC.* September 8, 2021. https://www.cnbc.com/2021/09/08/post-covid-just-7-percent-of-workers-say-they-have-a-dream-job-.html.

Dixon, Claire Kittle. 2015. "Choose A Job You Love: Maybe Confucius Was Right." *America's Future.* August 12, 2015. https://americasfuture.org/choose-a-job-you-love-maybe-confucius-was-right.

O'Donnell, J.T. 2018. "This is the No. 1 Reason Why People Fail at Switching Jobs (and What to Do About It)." *Inc.* February

14, 2018. https://www.inc.com/jt-odonnell/this-is-no-1-reason-why-people-fail-at-switching-jobs-and-what-to-do-about-it.html.

Peterson, Michael. 2023. *From Business Professional to Business Professor.* Self-published.

CHAPTER 7:

Consumer Finance. 2022. "Understanding paycheck deductions." *Consumer Finance.* Summer 2022. https://files.consumerfinance.gov/f/documents/cfpb_building_block_activities_understanding-paycheck-deductions_handout.pdf.

De La Rosa, Wendy. 2021. "10 steps to boost your financial health—that you can do in a day." Filmed March 3, 2021, in Philadelphia, PA. TED video, 3:26. https://www.youtube.com/watch?v=NmV5UIdIsQI.

Grabmeier, Jeff. 2021. "Husbands still seen as the experts on their household's finances." *Ohio State University.* April 12, 2021. https://news.osu.edu/husbands-still-seen-as-the-experts-on-their-households-finances.

Levitt, Aaron. 2022. "Why Should I Pay Myself First?" *Investopedia.* March 22, 2022. https://www.investopedia.com/ask/answers/12/pay-yourself.asp.

Moss, Wes. 2022. *What the Happiest Retirees Know.* US: McGraw Hill.

Obama Speeches. 2005. *American Legion Legislative Rally Remarks by Senator Barack Obama.* March 1, 2005. http://obamaspeeches.com/007-American-Legion-Legislative-Rally-Obama-Speech.htm

O'Shea, Arielle. 2022. "How Much Should You Save for Retirement?" *Nerd Wallet.* April 5, 2022. https://www.nerdwallet.com/article/investing/how-much-to-save-for-retirement.

Smalley, Cassandra, 2023. *The Why of Wealth*. US: New Degree Press.

Sonenshine, Jacob. 2017. "The reasons most couples fight about money." *New York Post*. August 3, 2017. https://nypost.com/2017/08/03/the-reasons-most-couples-argue-about-money.

SSA (Social Security Administration). n.d. "Contribution and Benefit Base." Accessed October 2022. https://www.ssa.gov/oact/cola/cbb.html.

Taylor, Jennifer. 2022. "15 Most Important Assets That Will Increase Your Net Worth." *Go Banking Rates*. October 20, 2022. https://www.gobankingrates.com/money/financial-planning/important-assets-increase-money.

Tumulty, Karen. 2022. "Personal finance class should be required in high school." *Washington Post*. June 12, 2022. https://www.washingtonpost.com/opinions/2022/06/12/personal-finance-class-should-be-required-high-school.

CHAPTER 8:

Algar, Selim. 2022. "Florida to require high school financial literacy course to graduate." *New York Post*. March 22, 2022. https://nypost.com/2022/03/22/florida-to-require-high-school-financial-literacy-class.

Allende, Isabelle. 2014. "How to Live Passionately—No Matter What Your Age." Filmed September 3, 2014, in Vancouver, Canada. TED video, 8:21. https://www.youtube.com/watch?v=5ifMRNag2XU.

Bodnar, Janet. 2022. "How to Retire With No Regrets." *Kiplinger's Personal Finance Magazine*. December 2022.

Brandon, Emily. 2022. "The Most Popular Ages to Collect Social Security." *U.S. News & World Report*. January 22, 2022. https://money.usnews.com/money/retirement/social-security/articles/the-most-popular-ages-to-collect-social-security.

Conde, Arturo. 2022. "T. Rowe Price Has Identified Two Types of Retirees: Which Type Are You?" *Smart Asset*. March 26, 2022. https://smartasset.com/retirement/retirement-savings-and-withdrawal-strategies.

Fernando, Jason. 2022. "The Power of Compound Interest: Calculations and Examples." *Investopedia*. July 19, 2022. https://www.investopedia.com/terms/c/compoundinterest.asp.

Geier, Ben. 2021. "One-Third of American Workers Are Leaving Free Money on the Table." *Smart Asset*. August 10, 2021. https://smartasset.com/retirement/one-third-of-american-workers-are-leaving-free-money-on-the-table.

Rampton, John. 2022. "101 Must-Know Retirement Statistics for 2022." *Retirement* (blog) *Due*. May 25, 2022. https://due.com/blog/retirement-statistics.

Telerski, Dylan. 2022. "How Much Do Companies Typically Match on 401(k) in 2022?" *My Ubiquity. March 9, 2022.* https://www.myubiquity.com/business/average-company-401k-match-in-2022.

White, Elizabeth. 2018. "An honest look at the personal financial crisis." Filmed July 12, 2018, in Richmond, VA. TED video, 18:03. https://www.ted.com/talks/elizabeth_white_an_honest_look_at_the_personal_finance_crisis.

CHAPTER 9:

Allende, Isabel. 2014. "How to Live Passionately—No Matter Your Age." Filmed September 3, 2014, in Vancouver, Canada. TED video, 8:06. https://www.ted.com/talks/isabel_allende_how_to_live_passionately_no_matter_your_age.

Curry, Benjamin. 2022. "Early Retirement Guide." *Forbes*. July 8, 2022. https://www.forbes.com/advisor/retirement/guide-to-early-retirement.

Davis, Kylee. 2021. "Higher Education E-Portfolio Personal Statement." *LinkedIn.* June 2021. https://www.linkedin.com/in/kylee-davis-46187ab2.

Jenkins, Jo Ann. 2021. "It's Time to Rethink Aging and Retirement." *Barrons.* May 17, 2021. https://www.barrons.com/articles/rethink-aging-retirement-51621024227.

RBC Wealth Management. 2019. "Will you outlive your money in retirement? 3 risks to plan for now." *RBC Wealth Management.* June 2019. https://www.rbcwealthmanagement.com/en-us/insights/will-you-outlive-your-money-in-retirement-3-risks-to-plan-for-now.

Sinykin, Aaron. 2021. "At What Point Is Someone Considered Elderly?" *Devoted Guardians. April 21,* 2021. https://devoted-guardians.com/at-what-point-is-someone-considered-elderly.

Suknanan, Jasmin. 2022. "Here's the average 401(k) balance of Americans in their 50s and 60s—how do you compare?" *CNBC.* April 25, 2022. https://www.cnbc.com/select/average-401k-balance-of-americans-in-50s-and-60s.

CHAPTER 10:

CDC (Centers for Disease Control). n.d. "Underlying Cause of Death, 1999–2018." Accessed May 2022. https://wonder.cdc.gov/ucd-icd10.html.

Dorris, Bruce. 2022. "Occupational Fraud 2022: A Report to the Nations." *ACFE.* June 2022. https://acfepublic.s3.us-west-2.amazonaws.com/2022+Report+to+the+Nations.pdf.

Mayo Clinic. 2022. "Chemotherapy." *Mayo Clinic.* March 22, 2022. https://www.mayoclinic.org/tests-procedures/chemotherapy/about/pac-20385033.

McInerny, Nora. 2019. "We don't 'move on' from grief. We move forward with it." Filmed April 9, 2019, in Palm Springs, CA.

TED video, 14:50. https://www.ted.com/talks/nora_mcinerny_we_don_t_move_on_from_grief_we_move_forward_with_it.

NBCF (National Breast Cancer Foundation). 2020. "What Does it Mean to Have Sage 2 Breast Cancer?" April 15, 2020. https://www.nationalbreastcancer.org/breast-cancer-stage-2.

Virani, Salim. 2021. "Heart Disease and Stroke Statistics—2021 update." *American Heart Association.* February 23, 2021. https://www.ahajournals.org/doi/10.1161/CIR.0000000000000950.

Weisbrot, Eric. 2022. "35+ Shocking Employee Theft Statistics to Know in 2022." *JW Surety Bonds.* January 15, 2022. https://www.jwsuretybonds.com/blog/employee-theft-statistics.

CHAPTER 11:

Crone, Emily Starbuck. 2021. "Jumbo Loans: When a Regular Mortgage Isn't Enough." *Nerdwallet.* December 3, 2021. https://www.nerdwallet.com/article/mortgages/jumbo-loans-what-you-need-to-know.

Emrath, Paul. 2021. "Second Homes: 15 Percent of New Home Sales." *Eye on Housing.* March 18, 2021. https://eyeonhousing.org/2021/03/second-homes-15-percent-of-new-home-sales.

Fontinelle, Amy. 2022. "Do-It-Yourself Projects to Boost Home Value." *Investopedia.* August 5, 2022. https://www.investopedia.com/articles/mortgages-real-estate/08/diy-home-projects.asp.

Juarez, Alexis. 2020. "Tips to Help You Ace Your First Job Interview After College." Streamed live on October 26, 2020. YouTube video, 3:18. https://www.youtube.com/watch?v=GaNWflcXXag.

Katz, David. 2002. "The Big Eight: Consolidation and scandal did in the big eight group of accounting firms." *CFO.* December 31, 2002. https://www.cfo.com/accounting-tax/2002/12/the-big-eight-8553.

Pruthi, Sandhya. 2021. "Stress Relief from Laughter? It's No Joke." *Mayo Clinic.* July 29, 2021. https://www.mayoclinic.org/

healthy-lifestyle/stress-management/in-depth/stress-relief/
art-20044456.

Wood, Kate. 2021. "What to Know About Buying a Second Home."
Nerdwallet. April 19, 2021. https://www.nerdwallet.com/article/
mortgages/buying-second-home.

CHAPTER 12:

Brooks, Authur. 2022. "10 Practical Ways to Improve Happiness."
The Atlantic. April 21, 2022. https://www.theatlantic.com/fam-
ily/archive/2022/04/happiness-research-how-to-be-happy-ad-
vice/629559.

Ingraham, David. 2022. "New data shows Americans more
miserable than we've been in half a century." *The Why Axis.*
January 28, 2022. https://thewhyaxis.substack.com/p/new-da-
ta-shows-americans-more-miserable.

Joy, Rebeccca. 2020. "The 9 Best Benefits of Playing Chess." *Health-
line.* October 5, 2020. https://www.healthline.com/health/ben-
efits-of-playing-chess#elevates-creativity.

Markushan, Yury. 2011. "40 Facts About Chess Most People Don't
Know." *Chess World.* November 17, 2011. https://thechessworld.
com/articles/general-information/40-facts-about-chess-most-
people-dont-know.

Price, Dominic. 2021. "What's your happiness score?" Filmed May
2021 in Sydney, Australia. TED video, 14:46. https://www.you-
tube.com/watch?v=ejQsLQvfnX4.

Ralphael, Isabel. 2020. "10 Oldest Baseball Stadiums in the US."
Parade. January 24, 2020. https://parade.com/146319/irapha-
el/10-oldest-ballparks-usa.

Printed in Great Britain
by Amazon